Common CORE Comprehension

D0800415

Practice at 3 Levels ●●●

Table of Contents

Using This Book

What Is the Common Core?

The Common Core State Standards are an initiative by states to set shared, consistent, and clear expectations of what students are expected to learn. This helps teachers and parents know what they need to do to help students. The standards are designed to be rigorous and pertinent to the real world. They reflect the knowledge and skills that our young people need for success in college and careers.

What Are the Intended Outcomes of Common Core?

The goal of the Common Core Standards is to facilitate the following competencies. Students will:

- demonstrate independence;
- build strong content knowledge;
- respond to the varying demands of audience, task, purpose, and discipline;
- comprehend as well as critique;
- value evidence;
- use technology and digital media strategically and capably;
- come to understand other perspectives and cultures.

What Does This Mean for You?

If your state has joined the Common Core State Standards Initiative, then as a teacher you are required to incorporate these standards into your lesson plans. Your students may need targeted practice in order to meet grade-level standards and expectations, and thereby be promoted to the next grade. This book is appropriate for on-grade-level students as well as intervention, ELs, struggling readers, and special needs students. To see if your state has joined the initiative, visit http://www.corestandards.org/in-the-states.

What Does the Common Core Say Specifically About Reading?

For reading, the Common Core sets the following key expectations.

- Students must read a "staircase" of increasingly complex texts in order to be ready for the demands of college or career-level reading.
- Students must read a diverse array of classic and contemporary literature from around the world, as well as challenging informational texts in a range of subjects.
- Students must show a "steadily growing ability" to comprehend, analyze, and respond critically to three main text types: Argument/Opinion, Informational, and Narrative.

Common Core Comprehension Grade 5 • ©2012 Newmark Learning, LLC

How Does This Book Help My Students?

Common Core Comprehension offers:

- **Three leveled, reproducible versions of each passage** are provided so that below-grade-level students start their comprehension practice at their reading level. Repeated readings and teacher support scaffold students up to the on-grade-level passage. Struggling students do not miss out on essential comprehension practice because the comprehension questions can be answered no matter which passage is read. The Common Core Standards require students to progress to grade-level competency. Therefore, it is recommended that once students build background on the topic, they staircase up to the on-grade-level passage, which includes richer vocabulary and language structures.

  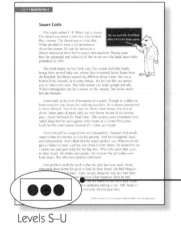

Levels N–P   Levels Q–R   Levels S–U

Gives the teacher the reading level of each of the three passages. See the chart on page 5.

- **An Overview page** introduces each of the three sections and provides background on the text type and genres in that section. A graphic organizer is provided to help you introduce the text type.

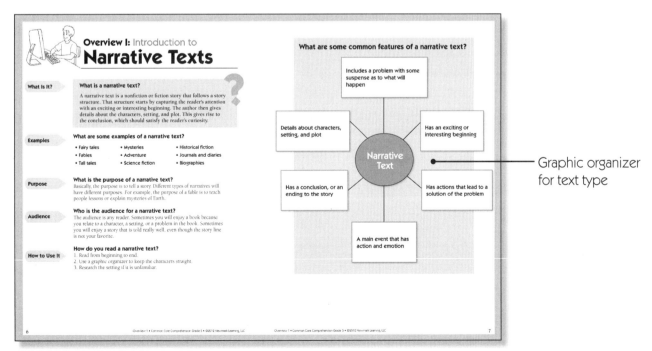

Graphic organizer for text type

Introductory spread

- **Each set of passages in a genre begins with a mini-lesson** that consistently frames the specific details of the genre students are about to read. A reproducible graphic organizer is provided for you to share as is, or you can cover the answers and complete together or individually as a response to your mini-lesson.

Explanation of the genre   Graphic organizer to copy or project

Brief explanation of how this text is different from other types of text

Gives a purpose for this genre

Notes the audience for this type of text

Tips for comprehending this type of text

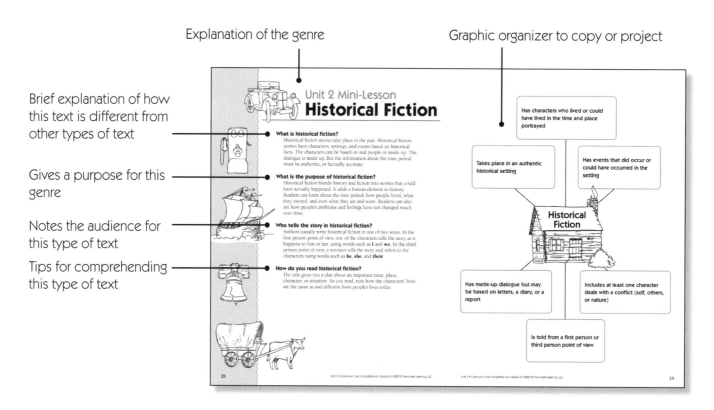

- **Text-dependent and critical-thinking questions** appear after each set of passages. The questions are research based and support the Common Core reading standards at grade level.

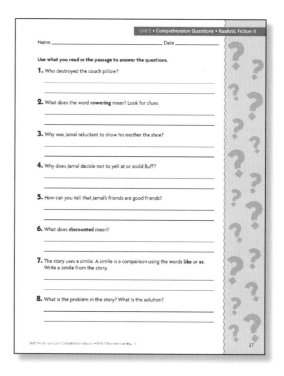

- **Students get rich text type and genre practice** using an array of narrative texts, content-area informational texts in social studies and science, and opinion/argument texts, as per the Common Core Standards.

Narrative Texts

Informational Texts

Opinion/Argument Texts

- **Vocabulary is studied in context,** as per the Common Core Standards.

> That morning, Jamal had put away everything a dog might want to chew. But Buff still found something to destroy.
>
> "Buff! There you are!" yelled Jamal. He found Buff hiding behind a bed. Jamal dropped to his knees beside Buff. Buff was **cowering**, or shaking with fear. "It's all right, boy. I'm not going to yell at you." Jamal had already tried yelling. It didn't work. "I just want to know why you keep doing this. You know it will get you into trouble."

How Are the Passages Leveled?

The first passage is two grades below level, the second passage is one grade below level, and the third passage is on grade level. Please refer to the chart below to see a correlation to letter levels and number levels.

Common Core Practice Reading Levels

Level Icon	Grade 1		Grade 2		Grade 3		Grade 4		Grade 5		Grade 6	
●○○	A–C	1–4	D–E	5–8	F–I	9–16	L–M	24–28	N–P	30–38	Q–R	40
●●○	D–E	5–8	F–I	9–16	J–M	18–28	N–P	30–38	Q–R	40	S–U	44–50
●●●	F–I	9–16	J–M	18–28	N–P	30–38	Q–R	40	S–U	44–50	V–X	60

Overview 1: Introduction to **Narrative Texts**

What Is It?

What is a narrative text?

A narrative text is a nonfiction or fiction story that follows a story structure. That structure starts by capturing the reader's attention with an exciting or interesting beginning. The author then gives details about the characters, setting, and plot. This gives rise to the conclusion, which should satisfy the reader's curiosity.

Examples

What are some examples of a narrative text?

- Adventure
- Biographies
- Fables
- Fairy tales
- Historical fiction
- Journals and diaries
- Mysteries
- Science fiction
- Tall tales

Purpose

What is the purpose of a narrative text?

Basically, the purpose is to tell a story. Different types of narratives will have different purposes. For example, the purpose of a fable is to teach people lessons or explain mysteries of Earth.

Audience

Who is the audience for a narrative text?

The audience is any reader. Sometimes you will enjoy a book because you relate to a character, a setting, or a problem in the book. Sometimes you will enjoy a story that is told really well, even though the story line is not your favorite.

How to Use It

How do you read a narrative text?

1. Read from beginning to end.
2. Use a graphic organizer to keep the characters straight.
3. Research the setting if it is unfamiliar.

What are some common features of a narrative text?

Includes a problem with some suspense as to what will happen

Details about characters, setting, and plot

Has an exciting or interesting beginning

Narrative Text

Has a conclusion, or an ending to the story

Has actions that lead to a solution of the problem

A main event that has action and emotion

Unit 1 Mini-Lesson
Memoir/Personal Narrative

What is a memoir?

A memoir is writing that covers a short period of time in the life of the person writing it. Memoirs focus on the events, thoughts, and feelings of that person. They are often about a specific time or place, or a moment in history that is important to the writer.

What is the purpose of a personal memoir?

The purpose of a memoir is to describe events as the writer remembers them. These writers want to share their experiences with the rest of the world. Writers may also use the memoir as a journey of self-discovery. Writing about the past can help people better understand themselves and how they came to be who they are.

Who writes memoirs?

In the past, people who took part in world-changing events, like explorations or scientific discoveries, wrote memoirs. The writers wanted to give an eyewitness account of the event. But memoirs are not always about major or public events.

How do you read a memoir?

When you read a memoir, you are reading a first-person narrative: one person's memory of an event or time. Enter into the moment with the writer. Try to picture yourself there. Think about what is important and why the writer chose to write about the event.

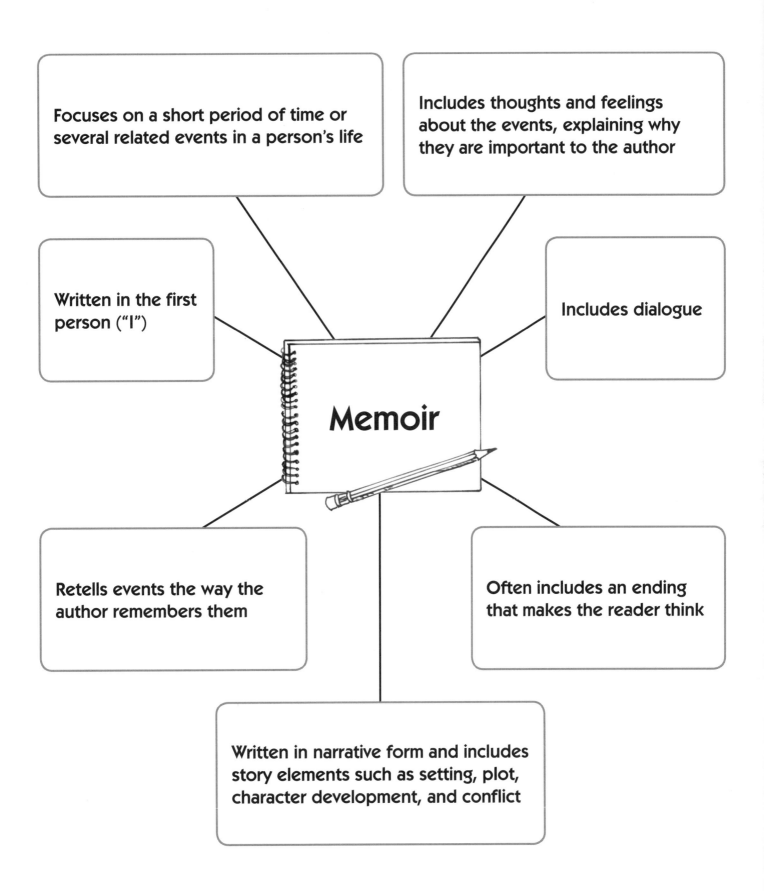

Focuses on a short period of time or several related events in a person's life

Includes thoughts and feelings about the events, explaining why they are important to the author

Written in the first person ("I")

Includes dialogue

Memoir

Retells events the way the author remembers them

Often includes an ending that makes the reader think

Written in narrative form and includes story elements such as setting, plot, character development, and conflict

Bienvenido a Nueva York

I was ten years old in 1937. That's when my brother Nicky and I got exciting and scary news. Our father was sending money to my aunts, Tía Manuela and Tía Rosa. *Tía* means "aunt" in Spanish. The money was for us to go to New York. We were going to live with our father! We would go to New York on a boat. Airplanes were only for rich people. I was petrified of the trip. Petrified means very scared. What if the boat sank? I didn't know how to swim very well.

I didn't know my mother and father. They had moved to New York City when I was two years old. They moved there to find work so they could take care of our family. Since then they had divorced. My brother Nicky and I lived with my father's younger sisters, Tía Rosa and Tía Manuela. Nicky is two years older than me. Our home was in San Juan. San Juan is the biggest city in Puerto Rico. We lived together in a one-room apartment. The apartment had cracking walls and peeling paint. There was one bathroom and shower in the building. All of the tenants shared the bathroom. Tenants are people who lived in a building. I thought everybody lived like this.

Finally, the day came for us to go to New York. It was Nicky, me, and Tía Manuela. Tía Rosa would come to New York a few years later. It was hard to say good-bye to our friends. But I was still thinking about the boat. What would I do if it sank? I don't remember how many days we were on the boat. I spent the whole trip in my bed. I was seasick. I threw up over and over again. I was happy when the boat finally got to New York.

We walked off the boat carrying our valises. A valise is a suitcase. A friendly looking, but strange man was waving to us. "Es su papá," Tía Manuela whispered to Nicky and me. That means "It's your father." My father? We waved back. We were excited. I spoke only Spanish. I didn't know many English words. I would have to learn a new language. I felt nervous and scared again.

My father's apartment was on West 116th Street and Eighth Avenue. When I walked in, I was spellbound. **Spellbound** means amazed. The apartment had a kitchen, a bedroom, a living room, electric lights, and its own bathroom! I was amazed that only one family would be living in such a huge place! We had a lot to get used to. The best part was that we would be living with our papá!

Bienvenido a Nueva York

In the summer of 1937, my brother Nicky and I got exciting and scary news. My father was sending money to my aunts, Tía Manuela and Tía Rosa. The money was for us to move to New York and live with him! We would travel to New York on a boat. Traveling by airplane was something only wealthy people did. I was happy to go live in New York, but I was petrified, or very scared, of the sea trip. What if the boat sank? I didn't know how to swim very well.

I was ten years old, but I didn't know my mother and father. They had moved to New York City when I was two years old. They moved there to find work and support our family. Since then they had divorced. I lived with my father's younger sisters, my aunts Tía Rosa and Tía Manuela, and my brother, Nicolas. Nicolas is two years older than me. Our home was in San Juan, the biggest city in Puerto Rico. We squeezed together in a one-room apartment with cracking walls and peeling paint. There was one bathroom and shower in the building, which all the tenants shared. As bad as this sounds, I thought everybody lived this way.

Finally, the day came for Nicky, me, and Tía Manuela to begin our trip. (Tía Rosa wouldn't come to New York for a few more years.) It was hard to say good-bye to our friends. But I was still thinking about the boat. What would I do if it sank? I spent the whole voyage seasick in my small bed. I threw up over and over again. I was happy when the boat finally docked in Manhattan. I was in New York!

We walked off the boat carrying our valises, or suitcases. I saw a friendly looking, but strange man waving to us from behind a fence. "Es su papá," Tía Manuela whispered. My father? We waved back excitedly. I spoke only Spanish. I didn't know many English words. I would have to learn a new language. I felt nervous and scared again.

My father's apartment was on West 116th Street and Eighth Avenue. When I walked in, I was spellbound. I couldn't believe it. The apartment had a kitchen, a bedroom, a living room, electric lights, and its own bathroom! I was amazed that only one family would be living in such a huge place! We had a lot to get used to, but the best part was that we would be living with our papá!

Bienvenido a Nueva York

In the summer of 1937, my brother Nicky and I got exciting and scary news. My father was sending money to my aunts, Tía Manuela and Tía Rosa. The money was for us to move to New York and live with him! We would travel to New York on a boat. Traveling by airplane was something only wealthy people did. I was happy to go live in New York, but I was petrified, or very scared, of the sea trip. What if the boat sank? I didn't know how to swim very well.

I was ten years old, but I didn't know my mother and father. They had moved to New York City when I was two years old. They had moved there to find work and support our family. Since then they had divorced. I lived with my father's younger sisters, my aunts Tía Rosa and Tía Manuela, and my brother, Nicolas. Nicolas is two years older than me. Our home was in San Juan, the biggest city in Puerto Rico. We squeezed together in a one-room apartment with cracking walls and peeling paint. There was one bathroom and shower in the building, which all the tenants shared. As bad as this sounds, I thought everybody lived this way.

Finally, the August day came for Nicky, me, and Tía Manuela to begin our trip. (Tía Rosa wouldn't come to New York for another few years.) It was hard to say good-bye to our friends and neighbors. But I was still thinking about the boat. What would I do if it sank? I don't remember how many days we were on the boat. That's because I spent the whole voyage seasick in my small bed. I threw up over and over again. I was happy when the boat finally arrived and docked in Manhattan. I was in New York!

We walked off the boat carrying our valises, or suitcases. I saw a friendly looking, but strange man waving to us from behind a fence. "Es su papá," Tía Manuela whispered. My father? We waved back excitedly. I spoke only Spanish. I didn't know many English words. I would have to learn a new language. I felt nervous and scared again.

My father's apartment was on West 116th Street and Eighth Avenue. When I walked in, I was spellbound. I couldn't believe it. The apartment had a kitchen, a bedroom, a living room, electric lights, and its own bathroom! I was amazed that only one family would be living in such a huge place! We had a lot to get used to, but the best part was that we would be living with our papá!

Name _____ Date _____

Use what you read in the passage to answer the questions.

1. Why is the news from the writer's father both exciting and scary?

_____

_____

2. In what state does the story take place?

_____

_____

3. Why doesn't the family take an airplane to New York?

_____

_____

4. Why is the writer scared about taking a boat?

_____

_____

5. Why doesn't the writer know his mother and father?

_____

_____

6. What is another word for **spellbound**?

_____

_____

7. How is the apartment in New York different from the one in Puerto Rico?

_____

_____

8. Why doesn't the writer recognize his father?

_____

_____

Submarine Attack!

On Sunday morning, I read the news on the ship's bulletin board. Great Britain and Germany were at war! A lifeboat drill was scheduled before noon. A lifeboat drill is when you practice in case of an emergency.

At the time, I was a 23-year-old American woman who had been working in London. The city was frantically preparing for war. I didn't want to leave, but I had to go home to America. I booked my transatlantic journey. **Transatlantic** means across the Atlantic Ocean. I would travel on the *Athenia*, a ship. It had left Liverpool the day before. There were 1,102 passengers and a crew of 315 on board.

Passengers joked nervously at the drill. "Don't worry. In another ten hours, we'll be too far out for submarines to follow. Let's celebrate."

I was expecting a happy evening. But as we were eating dessert, we heard a loud bang. At 7:40 P.M. on Sunday, September 3, 1939, my world changed. There was no alarm to warn us. The explosion sounded like a huge steel door slamming shut. The ship suddenly moved forward, causing dishes to crash on the floor. People screamed. The floor was filled with scrambling legs and feet. The *Athenia* had been torpedoed, or hit, by a Nazi submarine. A submarine is a ship that travels underwater.

I stumbled from the table toward the staircase. I was dragged and pushed by bodies. They were pressed close against me. The air was filled with thick, lung-choking soot, or powder. A huge cloud of black smoke hung over the water. People rushed in all directions. A stewardess handed me a life jacket and a blanket, but I said no. I knew other people needed them more, such as older people and those with children.

Our lifeboat landed with a splash. I felt the water moving beneath our boat. We slid away from the ship's side. We rowed up and down the choppy seas for more than seven hours. Finally, at 3 A.M., we saw lights through the darkness. It was an American ship called *City of Flint*. It had gotten the *Athenia's* signal for help. Soon crew members from the *Flint* dropped a long, scary ladder down the ship's side. I climbed the ladder without looking up or down. Strong arms pulled me onto the *City of Flint's* deck. I was aboard an American ship. I was safe. My whole life was ahead of me.

Submarine Attack!

On Sunday morning, I read the news on the ship's bulletin board. Great Britain and Germany were at war! A lifeboat drill, or practice, was scheduled before noon. At the time, I was a 23-year-old American woman who had been working in London. The city was frantically preparing for war. I didn't want to leave, but I had to go home to America. I booked my transatlantic journey across the ocean. I would travel on the *Athenia*, an ocean liner, or ship. It had left Liverpool the day before. There were 1,102 passengers and a crew of 315 on board the *Athenia*.

At the drill, passengers joked nervously. "Don't worry. In another ten hours, we'll be too far out for submarines to follow. Let's celebrate at dinner."

I wore my best dress and shoes, expecting a happy evening. Then as I was eating dessert we heard a very loud bang. At 7:40 P.M. on Sunday, September 3, 1939, my world changed forever. The explosion sounded like an enormous steel door slamming shut. The deafening sound of a dead weight hitting the ship was followed by noisy confusion. The ship lurched, or moved suddenly. This caused dishes to crash on the floor. Glasses and silverware slid off the tables. People screamed. The *Athenia* had been torpedoed, or hit, by a Nazi submarine.

I stumbled from the table toward the staircase. I was dragged and pushed by bodies pressed close against me. The air was filled with thick, lung-choking soot, or smoke. It was still light outside when I reached the deck. A huge cloud of black smoke hung over the water. People rushed in all directions. A stewardess handed me a life jacket and a blanket, but I refused. Other people, such as those with children, needed them more.

Our lifeboat landed with a splash. I felt the water moving underneath as we slid away from the ship's side. We rowed up and down the choppy seas for more than seven hours. We were scared, yet somehow calmed by a sense of determination. Finally at 3 A.M., we saw lights through the murky darkness. The American ship *City of Flint* had gotten the *Athenia*'s distress signal, or signal for help. Soon crew members from the *Flint* began to drop a long, scary ladder down the ship's side. Being careful not to look up or down, I made the climb. Strong arms pulled me over the rail onto the *City of Flint*'s deck. I was safe aboard an American ship. My whole life lay ahead of me.

Submarine Attack!

On Sunday morning, I read the news on the ship's bulletin board. Great Britain and Germany were at war! A lifeboat drill was scheduled before noon. At the time, I was a 23-year-old American woman who had been working in London. The city, like the rest of Britain, was frantically preparing for war. Though I was reluctant to leave, I had to go home to America. I booked a transatlantic passage on the ocean liner *Athenia*, which had departed from Liverpool the day before. There were 1,102 passengers and a crew of 315 on board the *Athenia*.

At the drill, the other passengers joked nervously. "Don't worry," said one passenger. "In another ten hours, we'll be too far out for submarines to follow. Let's celebrate at dinner."

Anticipating a happy evening, I wore my best dress and shoes. Then, halfway through dessert at 7:40 P.M. on Sunday, September 3, 1939, my world changed forever. There was no warning. Just a crazy bang, an explosion like the slamming of an enormous steel bank vault door followed by utter pandemonium. The ship lurched. Dishes crashed to the floor. Glasses and silverware slid off the tables. The *Athenia* had been torpedoed by a Nazi submarine.

I stumbled from the table toward the staircase, dragged and pushed by bodies pressed close against me. The air was filled with thick, lung-choking soot. As I reached the deck, a huge cloud of black smoke hung over the water. People rushed in all directions. I refused the life jacket and blanket being handed out by the stewardess. Others, older people and those with children, needed them more.

Our lifeboat landed with a splash, and I felt the water moving underneath as we slid away from the ship. We rowed up and down the choppy seas for more than seven hours, scared to death, of course, yet somehow calmed by a sense of determination. Finally at 3 A.M., we saw lights pierce the murky darkness. The American freighter *City of Flint* had picked up the *Athenia's* distress signal. Soon crew members from the *Flint* began to drop a long, scary ladder down the freighter's side. Determined not to look up or down, I made the climb. Soon strong arms pulled me over the rail onto the *City of Flint's* deck. I was safe aboard an American ship. My whole life lay ahead of me.

●●●

Name _____ Date _____

Use what you read in the passage to answer the questions.

1. Why does the writer have to leave London?

_____

_____

2. What does **transatlantic** mean?

_____

_____

3. How many passengers are aboard the *Athenia*?

_____

_____

4. Why are the passengers nervous?

_____

_____

5. What causes the dishes to crash on the floor?

_____

_____

6. What does the writer do that lets you know she is a caring person?

_____

_____

7. How many hours is the writer in the lifeboat? What is the sea like?

_____

_____

8. How does the writer feel about having to climb the ladder? How can you tell?

_____

_____

Unit 2 Mini-Lesson
Realistic Fiction

What is realistic fiction?

Realistic fiction features characters and plots that could actually happen in everyday life. The settings are authentic—they are based on familiar places such as a home, school, office, or farm. The stories involve some type of conflict or problem. The conflict can be something a character faces within him or herself, an issue between characters, or a problem between a character and nature.

What is the purpose of realistic fiction?

Realistic fiction shows how people grow and learn, deal with successes and failures, make decisions, build relationships, and solve problems. In addition to making readers think and wonder, realistic fiction is entertaining. Most of us enjoy "escaping" into someone else's life for a while.

Who is the audience for realistic fiction?

Anyone is the audience for realistic fiction. Realistic fiction is especially enjoyable for readers who are interested in human thoughts, feelings, and experiences in a realistic place or circumstance.

How do you read realistic fiction?

First note the title. The title will give you a clue about an important character or conflict in the story. As you read, pay attention to the thoughts, feelings, and actions of the main characters. Note how the characters change from the beginning of the story to the end. Ask yourself: *What moves these characters to action? Can I learn something from their struggles?*

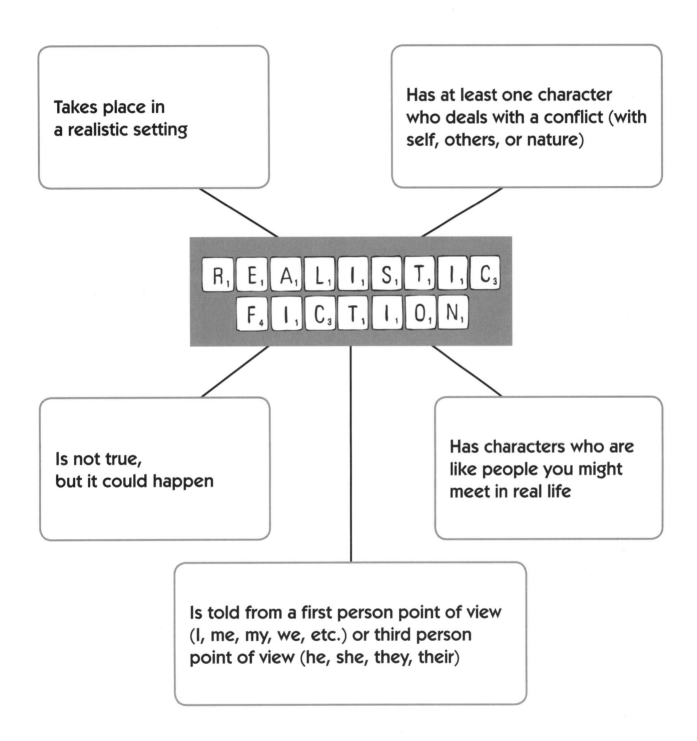

Takes place in a realistic setting

Has at least one character who deals with a conflict (with self, others, or nature)

REALISTIC FICTION

Is not true, but it could happen

Has characters who are like people you might meet in real life

Is told from a first person point of view (I, me, my, we, etc.) or third person point of view (he, she, they, their)

A Game Is a Game—Or Is It?

It was a rainy summer day. There was nothing to do but hang out at home. Cai and I were playing the game Scrabble®. On my porch Cai's dog Tucker was sleeping nearby, not far from Cai's feet. Tucker was tossing and turning and snorting and snoring. Jake and Linda walked by. They were wearing rain jackets. I guess they didn't notice us because Jake was speaking loudly. He said, "Cai is a terrible basketball player!"

I looked up to see if Cai was okay. He was. He ignored Jake's rudeness. "I'm a great basketball player," Jake was saying. "I have whirlwind moves."

"What is that supposed to mean?" asked Linda.

"It means my moves are strong and speedy. Playing against you is not a challenge. I've tried to teach you, Linda. But you don't listen!"

"Maybe I'd listen better if you'd stop yelling at me," Linda said.

"Well, anyway, I wish there were better players around," said Jake.

I could tell that Cai was beginning to feel sad. His shoulders slumped lower and lower. He moved closer to Tucker and petted him. I didn't know what to say to make him feel better. So I shouted at Jake. "Hey! We're right here, you know. "

Jake and Linda turned around quickly. Jake's eyes were wide. Cai spoke up. "Jake, we're playing Scrabble®. Would you like to play?" Sometimes I can't believe how nice Cai can be. Jake looked down at his feet. He mumbled, "No, thanks." But he didn't leave. He watched Cai, Linda, and me play.

"I'm terrible at board games," said Jake.

"Sit down. I'll teach you how to play," said Cai, smiling.

"Thanks," said Jake. "I'm really sorry about what I said."

"It's okay, Jake. Some people are good at board games and some people are good at basketball. But I think Maria and I are happy playing board games. We'll leave shooting baskets to you."

A Game Is a Game—Or Is It?

It was a dark, drizzly summer day. It was the kind of day when there's nothing to do but hang out at home. Cai and I were playing Scrabble® on my screened-in porch. Cai's dog Tucker was sleeping nearby. Tucker was tossing and turning and snorting and snoring. Jake and Linda strolled by in their rain jackets. I guess they didn't notice us because Jake was speaking loudly. He said, "Cai is a terrible basketball player!"

I looked up to see if Cai was okay. He was. He ignored Jake's rudeness and continued staring at the game board.

"I'm a great player," Jake was saying. "I have whirlwind moves."

"What is that supposed to mean?" asked Linda.

"It means my moves are forceful and speedy so that playing against you is easy. I've tried to teach you, Linda, but you don't listen!"

"Maybe I'd listen better if you'd stop yelling at me," Linda said.

I could tell that Cai was beginning to feel sad. His shoulders slumped lower and lower. He began to pet Tucker, like he does when he needs a friend. I didn't know what to say to make him feel better, so I shouted at Jake. "Hey! We're right here, you know."

Jake and Linda swung around. Jake's eyes were wide and embarrassed.

Cai spoke up. "Jake, we're playing Scrabble®. Would you like to play?" Sometimes I can hardly believe how nice Cai can be. Jake shuffled his feet and mumbled, "No, thanks." But he didn't leave. He watched Cai, Linda, and me play.

"I'm terrible at word games," said Jake.

"Sit down. I'll teach you how to play," said Cai, smiling.

"Thanks," said Jake, "and I'm really sorry about what I said."

"It's okay, Jake. Some people are good at board games and some are good at basketball. Don't take it personally, but I think Maria and I will happily stick to board games. We'll leave shooting baskets to you."

●●○   21

A Game Is a Game—Or Is It?

It was one of those dark, drizzly summer days when there's nothing to do but hang out at home. Cai and I were playing Scrabble® on my screened-in porch. His dog Tucker was sleeping nearby, tossing and turning and snorting and snoring. Jake and Linda strolled by in their rain jackets. I guess they didn't notice us because Jake said, in a very loud voice, "Cai is a terrible basketball player!"

I glanced up to see if Cai was okay; he was. He shrugged off Jake's rudeness and continued staring at the Scrabble® board.

"I'm a great basketball player," Jake was saying. "I have whirlwind moves so playing against you is no challenge. I've tried to teach you, Linda, but you don't listen!"

"Maybe I'd listen better if you'd stop yelling at me," Linda said.

I could tell that Cai was beginning to feel sad because his shoulders were slumping lower and lower. He began to pet Tucker, like he usually did when he needed a friend. I didn't know what to say so I shouted at Jake. "Hey! We're right here listening to everything you're saying."

Jake and Linda swung around. Jake's eyes were wide and embarrassed, but he didn't apologize. He just stood there, gaping at us.

Then Cai spoke up. "Jake, we're playing Scrabble®. Would you like to play?" Sometimes I can hardly believe how nice Cai can be. Jake shuffled his feet and mumbled, "No, thanks," but he didn't leave. He just stood there, watching, as Cai and Linda and I started to play.

"I'm terrible at word games," said Jake.

"Sit down. I'll teach you how to play," said Cai, smiling.

"Thanks," said Jake. "And hey, I'm really sorry about what I said."

"It's okay, Jake. Some people are good at board games and some people are good at basketball. Don't take it personally, but I think Maria and I will happily stick to board games and leave shooting baskets to you."

Name _____ Date _____

Use what you read in the passage to answer the questions.

1. Where and when does this story take place?

_____

_____

2. Who are the characters in this story?

_____

_____

3. Which character is telling the story?

_____

_____

4. What details describe Tucker sleeping?

_____

_____

5. What does the word **whirlwind** mean in this story?

_____

_____

6. What clues tell you that what Jake is saying makes Cai sad?

_____

_____

7. What clues help you infer that Jake is not a very good teacher?

_____

_____

8. How is the problem in this story solved?

_____

_____

Buff Goes Wild

White cotton fluff was everywhere. One of the pillows was now flat. It looked like an empty bag. "Oh no!" cried Jamal. Jamal shut the front door behind him. "Buff!" he called as he looked for his dog. It was the third day this week Buff had destroyed something.

Yesterday, Jamal's mom had said "Our apartment isn't very large." She said this after Jamal showed her a shoe Buff had chewed. He hadn't wanted to show it to her, but he did. "Maybe we should give Buff to a family with a yard."

Mom's comment made Jamal upset. His chest hurt. "This is the best home for Buff! We're his family!"

That morning, Jamal had put away everything a dog might want to chew. But Buff still found something to destroy.

"Buff! There you are!" yelled Jamal. He found Buff hiding behind a bed. Jamal dropped to his knees beside Buff. Buff was **cowering**, or shaking with fear. "It's all right, boy. I'm not going to yell at you." Jamal had already tried yelling. It didn't work. "I just want to know why you keep doing this. You know it will get you into trouble."

Jamal asked his friends what to do. "If I were Buff, I'd be really bored too," said his friend Luke. "This place is boring for a dog."

"Maybe that's the problem," said Jamal. "I just need to find him something to do."

""Buy Buff toys to keep him busy," Mia suggested. "I've got some money. I'll buy him a toy."

"Thanks!" Jamal said.

Their teacher walked the kids to the pet store. At the store, they bought all kinds of discounted dog toys. **Discounted** means they cost less money. The next morning before school, Jamal made sure Buff had all his new toys. After school, Jamal and his friends went to check on Buff. Thankfully, Buff had only chewed on his new chew toys!

Buff Goes Wild

"Oh no!" cried Jamal. "This is just great." White cotton fluff lay everywhere, like little clouds on the carpet. One of the pillows that usually sat on the couch was now flat. It looked like an empty sack laying on the floor. One corner had been chewed off.

Jamal stepped inside. He shut the front door behind him. "Buff!" he called as he looked for his dog. "Where are you?" It was the third day this week that Buff had destroyed something.

"Our apartment isn't very large," Jamal's mom had told him yesterday. She had just seen a shoe that Buff had chewed to bits. "We need to decide whether this is really the best home for a big dog. Maybe we should give Buff to a family with a yard."

That morning, Jamal had put away everything a dog might want to chew. But Buff had still found something to destroy.

"Buff! There you are!" Jamal said when he found Buff hiding behind a bed. Jamal dropped to his knees beside a cowering Buff. "It's all right, boy. I'm not going to yell at you." Jamal had already tried yelling, and it didn't work. "I just want to know why you keep doing this. You know it'll get you into trouble."

The next day, Jamal asked his friends what to do. "I feel bad for Buff," said Luke. "I'd be bored if it were me sitting around an apartment all day."

"Hey, maybe that's the problem," said Jamal. "I just need to find him something to do."

"Buy Buff some toys to keep him busy," Mia suggested. "I've got some money. I'll buy him a toy."

"Thanks!" Jamal said.

Their teacher, Ms. Tilly, agreed to walk the kids to the pet store. At the store, they bought an assortment of dog toys. They were all discounted, or on sale. The next morning before school, Jamal made sure Buff had all his new toys. After school, he and his friends were pleased. Buff had only chewed on his new toys!

Buff Goes Wild

White cotton fluff lay everywhere, like little clouds on the carpet. One of the throw pillows was now a flat, empty sack. It was laying in the middle of the floor. Jamal stepped inside, shutting the front door behind him. "Buff!" he called as he looked around for his dog. "Where are you?" It was the third day this week he'd come home to destruction.

"Our apartment isn't very large," Jamal's mom had told him yesterday. He had showed her a shoe that Buff had chewed to pieces. "Maybe we should give Buff to a family who has a yard." Jamal felt sick!

That morning, Jamal had carefully put away everything a dog might want to chew. But Buff had still found something to destroy.

"Buff! There you are!" Jamal said as he spotted Buff hiding behind a bed. Jamal dropped to his knees beside a cowering Buff. "It's all right, boy," he told the dog. "I'm not going to scold you." Jamal had already tried yelling, and it didn't work. "I just want to know why you keep doing this when you know it'll get you into trouble."

Jamal asked his friends what to do. "I feel bad for Buff," said Luke. "I'd be bored sitting around an apartment all day."

"Hey, maybe that's the problem," said Jamal. "Maybe Buff is bored. In that case, I just need to find him something to do."

"Buy Buff some toys to keep him busy," Mia suggested. "I've got some money. I'll buy him a toy."

"Thanks!" Jamal said gratefully.

Their teacher Ms. Tilly agreed to walk the kids to the pet store, where they purchased an assortment of discounted dog toys.

The next morning before leaving for school, Jamal made sure Buff had all his new toys with him. After school, he and his friends were pleasantly surprised. Buff had not chewed on anything but his new chew toys!

Name _____ Date _____

Use what you read in the passage to answer the questions.

1. Who destroyed the couch pillow?

_____

_____

2. What does the word **cowering** mean? Look for clues.

_____

_____

3. Why was Jamal reluctant to show his mother the shoe?

_____

_____

4. Why does Jamal decide not to yell at or scold Buff?

_____

_____

5. How can you tell that Jamal's friends are good friends?

_____

_____

6. What does **discounted** mean?

_____

_____

7. The story uses a simile. A simile is a comparison using the words **like** or **as**. Write a simile from the story.

_____

_____

8. What is the problem in the story? What is the solution?

_____

_____

Unit 3 Mini-Lesson
Historical Fiction

What is historical fiction?

Historical fiction stories take place in the past. Historical fiction stories have characters, settings, and events based on historical facts. The characters can be based on real people or made up. The dialogue is made up. But the information about the time period must be authentic, or factually accurate.

What is the purpose of historical fiction?

Historical fiction blends history and fiction into stories that could have actually happened. It adds a human element to history. Readers can learn about the time period: how people lived, what they owned, and even what they ate and wore. Readers can also see how people's problems and feelings have not changed much over time.

Who tells the story in historical fiction?

Authors usually write historical fiction in one of two ways. In the first person point of view, one of the characters tells the story as it happens to him or her, using words such as **I** and **we**. In the third person point of view, a narrator tells the story and refers to the characters using words such as **he**, **she**, and **their**.

How do you read historical fiction?

The title gives you a clue about an important time, place, character, or situation. As you read, note how the characters' lives are the same as and different from people's lives today.

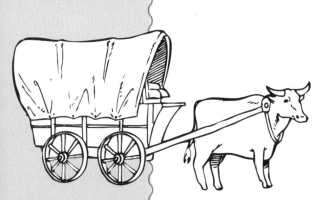

Has characters who lived or could have lived in the time and place portrayed

Takes place in an authentic historical setting

Has events that did occur or could have occurred in the setting

Historical Fiction

Has made-up dialogue but may be based on letters, a diary, or a report

Includes at least one character who deals with a conflict (self, others, or nature)

Is told from a first person or third person point of view

Blasting Through the Sierra Nevadas

Chang woke up suddenly. He heard a huge explosion. Chang jumped out of bed. He hurried toward the blast. Chang hurried to the Summit Tunnel. Chang and Wen had been neighbors in China. They had traveled together to the United States. They sold fireworks until they got jobs working on the railroad one year ago. It was the winter of 1867. Workers on the west coast were building a train track going east. From the east coast, workers were building the track going west. The two tracks would meet in Utah. The track had to go through the Sierra Nevada mountains. It was difficult and dangerous work. The workers had to cut into the mountain with axes and chisels in very cold weather. Chang saw Wen digging out three men. The men were stuck in the tunnel. The men had been trapped by the blast.

"What happened?" Chang asked.

Wen explained. There was a new engineer named James Howden. Howden had told the workers that he would blast through the rock using a compound, or combination, of chemicals. "Mr. Howden said he could control the blast. He was wrong."

When the men were rescued, Mr. Howden was holding a wooden box. "Who will take this new explosive into the tunnel?" No one volunteered. He said there was nothing to fear. The explosive was made of nitroglycerin. "I know what went wrong," Mr. Howden said. "I made a better fuse."

"If no one volunteers, I will choose someone," Mr. Howden said. "You," he said, pointing at Wen. "I saw how fast you worked to save those men. You will be able to place the explosive. Then you'll run out in time."

Wen's eyes were full of fear. Chang spoke to Mr. Howden. "Maybe we can wrap the explosive in a paper tube. We did that with fireworks in China. Then we can add a long fuse. This way the worker who sets it can light it and run."

"I see your point," Mr. Howden said. "Let's try it."

Chang was nervous. Very carefully, he lit the fuse. He ran as fast as he could. "It worked!" Chang said. The men cheered. Inside the tunnel, pieces of rock safely crumbled down.

Blasting Through the Sierra Nevadas

Chang woke up suddenly to the sound of a huge explosion. He jumped out of bed. He hurried toward the blast.

Chang hurried to the Summit Tunnel. Chang and his neighbor Wen had traveled together to the United States from China. They sold fireworks until they got jobs working on the Transcontinental Railroad one year ago. Now it was the winter of 1867. Workers on each coast were building train tracks that would meet in Utah. The track had to go through the Sierra Nevada mountains—difficult and dangerous work.

Wen was digging out three men when Chang got to the tunnel. The men had been trapped by the blast. Wen pulled aside large rocks.

"What happened?" Chang asked.

Wen explained that there was a new engineer named James Howden. Howden had told the workers that he would blast through the rock using a compound, or combination, of chemicals. When the men had been rescued, Mr. Howden held up a wooden box. "Who will take this new explosive into the tunnel?" No one volunteered.

He said there was no need to fear the nitroglycerin. "I know what went wrong," Mr. Howden said. "I made a better fuse. If no one volunteers, I will choose someone," Mr. Howden said. He pointed at Wen. "I saw how fast you worked to save those men. You will be able to place the explosive and run out in time."

Wen's eyes were full of fear. Chang spoke to Mr. Howden. "Maybe we can wrap the nitroglycerin in a paper tube. We did that with fireworks in China. Then we can add a long fuse. This way the worker who sets the blast will have time to escape."

"I see your point," Mr. Howden said to Chang. "Let's try it."

Chang was very nervous. Very carefully, he lit the fuse. He ran as fast as he could. *Boom!*

"It worked!" Chang said. The men cheered. Inside the tunnel, pieces of rock safely crumbled down.

Blasting Through the Sierra Nevadas

Chang was startled awake by a huge explosion. He jumped out of bed and hurried in the direction of the blast. Chang hurried to the Summit Tunnel. Chang and Wen had been neighbors in China and had traveled together to the United States. They sold fireworks until they found jobs working on the railroad one year ago. It was the winter of 1867. Workers on the west coast were building a train track going east. From the east, workers were building the track going west. The two tracks would meet in Utah. The track had to go through the Sierra Nevadas. But carving through mountains in the bitter cold with pickaxes was dangerous.

When Chang arrived at the tunnel, Wen was digging out three men. They had been trapped by the blast, and Wen was moving large rocks.

"What happened?" Chang asked.

"There is a new engineer named James Howden. He told the workers that he would use a compound, or combination, of chemicals to blast through the rock. He said he could control the blast, but he was wrong."

When the men were safe, Mr. Howden was holding a crate, or box. "Who will take this new explosive into the tunnel?" No one volunteered. He said there was no need to fear the nitroglycerin. Nitroglycerin was what the explosive was made of. "I know what went wrong," Mr. Howden said. "I made a better fuse. If no one volunteers, I will choose someone," Mr. Howden said. "You," he said, pointing at Wen. "I saw how fast you worked to save those men. You will be able to place the explosive and run out in time."

Chang had an idea of how to make the nitroglycerin blast safer. But he wasn't sure it would work. Chang spoke to Mr. Howden. "Maybe we can wrap the nitroglycerin in a paper tube, like we do with fireworks in China. Then we can add a long fuse. This way the worker who sets the blast will have more time before the chemicals explode."

"I see your point," Mr. Howden said. "Let's try it."

Chang was nervous. Very carefully, he lit the fuse, then ran as fast as he could. "It worked!" Chang said as the men cheered. Inside the tunnel, pieces of rock safely crumbled down.

Name _____ Date _____

Use what you read in the passage to answer the questions.

1. James Howden is an . . .

_____

_____

2. How do Wen and Chang know each other?

_____

_____

3. Where would the two railroad tracks meet?

_____

_____

4. In what way is the work dangerous?

_____

_____

5. What is a compound?

_____

_____

6. Why do you think Howden wants to blast the rock rather than carve, or cut, through it?

_____

_____

7. Why doesn't anyone volunteer to place the explosives in the tunnel?

_____

_____

8. How does Chang solve the problem?

_____

_____

Stable Boy at the Alamo

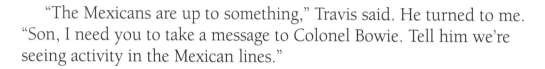

We had been trapped inside the fort for twelve days. The army of the Mexican general Santa Anna surrounded, or was around, the fort in San Antonio, Texas. I walked along the walls of the fort. I was looking at the campfires of the Mexican Army.

"I'm Jeremiah," said the guard on duty. Jeremiah told me that the Alamo, where we were, started out as a church. Around 1800, it was changed into a fort. High, two-foot-thick walls were built with adobe brick for protection and to hold cannons. I **proceeded**, or continued, to walk. I heard Bill Travis, our commander. He was talking to Davy Crockett, the famous frontiersman.

"The Mexicans are up to something," Travis said. He turned to me. "Son, I need you to take a message to Colonel Bowie. Tell him we're seeing activity in the Mexican lines."

"Yes, sir!" I said. Colonel Jim Bowie was very sick. I knocked on his door. I gave him the message about the attack. "Hand me those guns," said Bowie. "See my knife? Take it," Colonel Bowie said. "It won't do me much good in bed." I picked up the knife and hurried back.

When I got back to Colonel Travis and Davy Crockett, I heard gunshots ring out. I gathered the women and children and hid in the barracks. A loud banging erupted on the front door. Three soldiers in blue and red coats rushed in. They were Mexicans! I held my knife out. A man in a fancy uniform strode into the room. He looked at me. "I am Antonio López de Santa Anna," he said. "What is your name?"

"Harold Evans," I answered.

"You are holding a beautiful knife, Mr. Evans. May I see it?"

Here was my chance! I could kill Santa Anna. But . . . if I attacked him, it would put the others in danger. I handed the knife to him. "It's Jim Bowie's," I said.

Santa Anna looked at it. "It is yours now. You are a brave young man, Evans. You and these people may leave the fort safely." The soldiers put us in horse-drawn wagons. I looked down at the Bowie knife I had not used in my fight for independence.

Stable Boy at the Alamo

For the past twelve days, we had been trapped inside the fort. The army of the Mexican general Santa Anna surrounded the fort in San Antonio, Texas. I walked along the walls of the fort looking at the campfires of the Mexican Army. I said hello to the sentries, or soldiers, keeping watch.

"I'm Jeremiah," said a guard. Jeremiah told me that the Alamo started out as a church. Around 1800, it was changed into a fort. High, two-foot-thick walls were built with adobe brick for protection and to hold cannons. I proceeded, or continued, to walk along the walls of the Alamo. I heard Bill Travis talking to Davy Crockett.

"The Mexicans are up to something," Travis said. He turned in my direction. "Son, I need you to take a message to Colonel Bowie. Tell him we're seeing activity in the Mexican lines."

Jim Bowie was very sick. He stayed in his room. I knocked on his door. The colonel was in his bed. I gave him the message about the attack. "Hand me those guns," said Bowie. Beside the guns was a big hunting knife. "See my knife? Take it," Bowie said. "Won't do me much good in bed."

I picked up the knife and hurried back. When I got back to Colonel Travis and Davy Crockett, the sound of gunshots rang out. I gathered the women and children and ran to the barracks. Then a loud noise erupted from our barracks. Three soldiers in blue and red coats rushed in. They were Mexicans! A man in a fancy uniform strode into the room. "I'm Antonio López de Santa Anna," he said. "What's your name?"

"Harold Evans," I answered.

"You are holding a beautiful knife, Mr. Evans. May I see it?"

Here was my chance! I could kill Santa Anna. But . . . if I attacked him, it would put the others in danger. I handed the knife to him. "It's Jim Bowie's," I said. Santa Anna looked at it. "It is yours now. You are a brave young man, Evans. You and these people may leave the fort safely." The soldiers put us in horse-drawn wagons. I looked down at the Bowie knife I had not used in my fight for independence.

Stable Boy at the Alamo

For the past twelve days, we had been trapped inside the fort. The army of the Mexican general Santa Anna had surrounded the fort in San Antonio, Texas. I paced back and forth along the walls of the fort, looking at the campfires of the Mexican Army. I greeted the sentries keeping watch.

"I'm Jeremiah," said the guard. Jeremiah told me that the Alamo was originally a church. Around 1800, it was converted into a fort. High, two-foot-thick walls were built with adobe brick for protection and to hold cannons. I proceeded along the walls of the Alamo. I heard Bill Travis, our commander, talking to Davy Crockett, the famous frontiersman.

"The Mexicans are definitely planning something," Travis said. He swiveled in my direction. "Son, I need you to take a message to Colonel Bowie: tell him we're seeing increased activity in the Mexican lines."

"Yes, sir!" I said obediently. Colonel Jim Bowie was very sick and remained in his room. I knocked on his door and found the colonel in his bed. I gave him the message about the attack. "Hand me those guns," said Bowie, pointing to a pair of pistols. Beside them was a big hunting knife. "Take my knife," he said. "Won't do me much good in bed."

I picked up the knife and hurried back. When I got back to Colonel Travis and Davy Crockett, the sound of gunshots rang out. I gathered the women and children and hid in the barracks. Then three soldiers in blue and red coats rushed in carrying rifles. Mexicans! I pointed my knife as a man in a regal uniform strode in. "I am Antonio López de Santa Anna," he said to me. "What is your name?"

"I am Harold Evans," I answered boldly and proudly.

"You are holding a beautiful knife, Mr. Evans. May I see it?" Here was my chance! I could kill Santa Anna. But . . . if I attacked him, it would endanger the others. I handed the knife to him. "It's Jim Bowie's," I said.

Santa Anna looked at it. "It is yours now. You are a brave young man, Evans. You and these people may leave the fort safely." The soldiers put us in horse-drawn wagons. I looked down appreciatively at the Bowie knife that I had not used in my fight for independence.

●●●

Name _____ Date _____

Use what you read in the passage to answer the questions.

1. Who is Jeremiah?

_____

_____

2. Where does this story take place?

_____

_____

3. Who is invading the Alamo?

_____

_____

4. What was the Alamo before it was a fort?

_____

_____

5. What does **proceeded** mean?

_____

_____

6. Why is Jim Bowie in bed?

_____

_____

7. What clues tell you that Harold is a responsible person?

_____

_____

8. Why doesn't Harold kill Santa Anna?

_____

_____

Unit 4 Mini-Lesson
Science Fiction

What is science Fiction?

Science fiction stories use scientific facts and technological developments to imagine a world that doesn't yet exist—but could. Science fiction stories often take place in unusual settings, such as outer space, distant futures, or among alien creatures.

What is the purpose of science fiction?

Science fiction explores the benefits and dangers of technological advances.

Who invented science fiction?

Some say that science fiction was invented when someone imagined an alternate world or life on another planet. In the early 1700s, Jonathan Swift wrote about a world with only tiny beings. Since then, science fiction authors have written about time travel, visitors from other planets, robots, future societies, and the effect of computers and technology on human beings and the universe.

How do you read science fiction?

Look for science and technology words. Consider how these things are altering or changing the characters. Keep an open mind as you read. You are entering into a world of "what if." It might be a world of the future or the past. It might be on another planet or in another universe. It might even be a frightening world. But it is going to be an interesting trip!

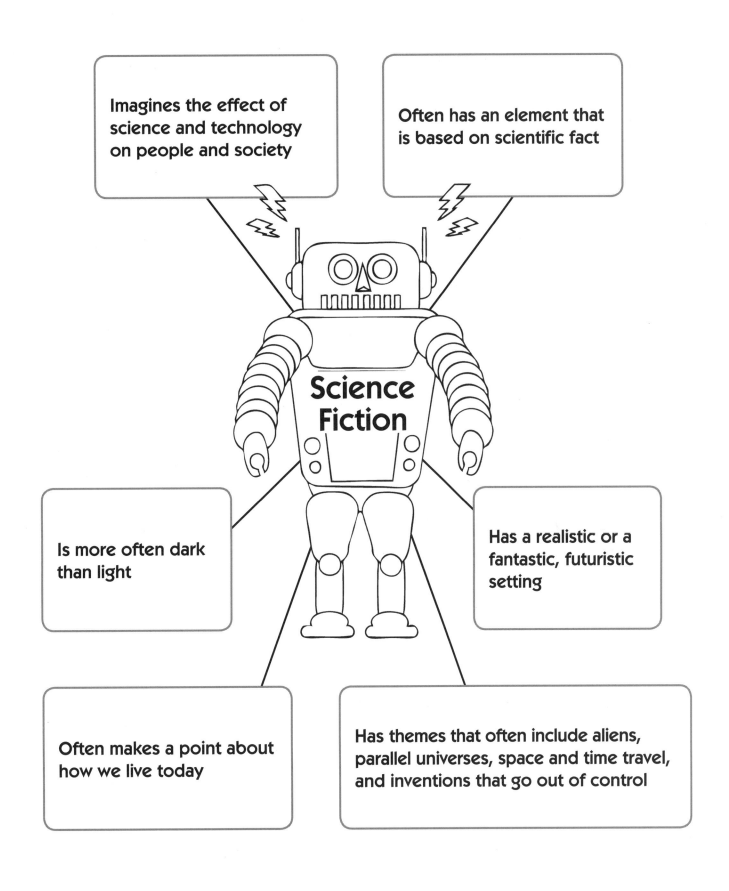

Imagines the effect of science and technology on people and society

Often has an element that is based on scientific fact

Science Fiction

Is more often dark than light

Has a realistic or a fantastic, futuristic setting

Often makes a point about how we live today

Has themes that often include aliens, parallel universes, space and time travel, and inventions that go out of control

Homework from the Future

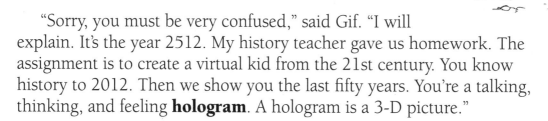

"Welcome to the future, CK-21. My name is Gif McCoy!"

"Huh? What? Where am I?" asked the CK-21.

"Sorry, you must be very confused," said Gif. "I will explain. It's the year 2512. My history teacher gave us homework. The assignment is to create a virtual kid from the 21st century. You know history to 2012. Then we show you the last fifty years. You're a talking, thinking, and feeling **hologram**. A hologram is a 3-D picture."

The CK-21 looked around. "This looks like the world before there were factories and machines. Everything is so green and beautiful. Something smells really good. I see the ocean! Where are we?"

"You're in Kansas!" said Gif. "You may be surprised to hear that Kansas has some of the world's most beautiful views of the ocean!"

"You can see the ocean from Kansas? Since when could you see the ocean?" The CK-21 could not believe it.

"Well, at the beginning of the 21st century, people knew using fossil fuels was heating up the planet. But people didn't stop. They just kept using up Earth's resources. Ice covering Earth melted. This caused its weight to move around. Volcanoes burst through Earth's crust in places where there never were volcanoes before," explained Gif. "In 2130, the oceans began to rise. They rose over farmland and cities. In 300 years, most of the eastern United States was covered in water. The only thing left were the Smokey Islands. You knew them as the Smokey Mountains."

"Oh," said the CK-21. The CK-21 was sad.

"Don't look so sad," said Gif. "People did end up learning from their mistakes. They decided to make sweeping changes. Today, there is less land and fewer people. But now we know how to use wind, solar, and hydroelectric power. Hydroelectric power is using water for electricity."

The CK-21 stared out at the waves. "I wonder why your teacher wanted you to show me this."

"You've got some homework to do, too," said Gif.

Homework from the Future

"Welcome to the future, CK-21. My name is Gif McCoy!"

"Huh? What? Where am I?" asked the confused CK-21.

"Sorry, you must be very confused," said Gif. "I will explain. It is the year 2512. My history teacher gave us some extracurricular homework. The assignment is to create a virtual 21st-century kid and show the kid what the year 2512 is like. You're a talking, thinking, and feeling hologram. That's a 3-D image. You're programmed to know about the world only up to the year 2012."

The CK-21 looked around with wonder. "This looks like the world before the Industrial Revolution, before machines and factories. Everything is so green and beautiful. Is that the ocean? Where are we?"

"You're in Kansas!" said Gif. "Kansas is home to some of the most beautiful ocean views and coastline in the world!"

"Kansas has ocean views? Since when?" asked the CK-21.

"Well, by the early 21st century, people knew that using lots of fossil fuels caused the planet to heat up. But people didn't stop. They just kept using up Earth's resources. Ice melted, its weight moved, and volcanic pressure burst through Earth's crust. There were volcanoes in places that never had them." Gif continued, "In 2130, the oceans began to rise. Oceans covered farmland and cities. In 300 years, most of the eastern United States was covered in water. All that remains are the Smokey Islands. You knew them as the Smokey Mountains."

"Oh," said the CK-21, sadly.

"Don't look so sad," said Gif. "People did end up learning from their mistakes and decided to innovate. Today, there is less land and fewer people, but now we know how to use wind, solar, and hydropower. This has allowed the planet to come back to life."

"I wonder why your teacher wanted you to show me this," said the CK-21.

"I think I have a good idea! You've got some homework too," Gif said.

Homework from the Future

"Welcome to the future, CK-21. My name is Gif McCoy!"

"Huh? What? Where am I?" asked the confused CK-21.

"Sorry, you must be very majorly confused," said Gif. "Allow me to explain. It's the year 2512, and my history teacher gave us some extracurricular homework. The assignment was to create a virtual 21st-century kid. Then I must show him or her around the year 2512. You're a talking, thinking, and feeling hologram—like a 3-D picture! I programmed you to only know about the world up to 2012."

The CK-21 looked around in amazement. "This looks like the world before the Industrial Revolution. Everything is so green and beautiful. I can smell something spectacular. Is that the ocean? Where are we?"

"You're in Kansas!" said Gif. "Kansas is home to some of the most beautiful ocean views and coastline in the world!"

"Kansas has ocean views?" asked the CK-21 in disbelief.

"Well, by the early 21st century, people knew that the massive use of fossil fuel was heating up the planet. But people didn't stop their destructive lifestyles. They just kept using up Earth's resources. The ice sheets melted, and Earth's crust shifted. Volcanic pressure burst through in places that never had volcanoes." Gif continued, "In 2130, the oceans began to rise over farmland and cities. In 300 years, most of the eastern United States was covered with water. All that remains are the Smokey Islands—formerly the Smokey Mountains."

"Oh," said the CK-21, sadly.

"Don't look so depressed," Gif said. "People did eventually learn from their mistakes and decided to make important changes. Today, we have less land, and fewer people. But we know how to use wind, solar, and hydropower efficiently. This has allowed the planet to come back to life."

The CK-21 stared out at the waves of the Eastern Ocean lapping at the Kansas coast. "I wonder why your teacher wanted you to show me this."

"I think I have an idea why! You've got some homework too." Gif said.

Name _____ Date _____

Use what you read in the passage to answer the questions.

1. What is the CK-21?

_____

_____

2. In what year does this story take place?

_____

_____

3. What is a **hologram**?

_____

_____

4. What is different about Kansas at this time in the future?

_____

_____

5. What caused all the problems on Earth?

_____

_____

6. What happened in 2130?

_____

_____

7. What were the Smokey Islands before?

_____

_____

8. How could the problems have been avoided?

_____

_____

App of the Year

Plexi's best friend, Benzo, won the galaxy's biggest prize: the App of the Year. Benzo's app was chosen to be a part of the E.T., or Everything Tech. All people lived with the E.T. from the time they were born.

The E.T. could do everything! The E.T. was your phone. It showed a hologram, or three-dimensional image, of the person you were talking to. The E.T. was your link to the Information Cloud. The Information Cloud could find out anything you wanted to know. The E.T. could not only do anything, but it could be anything. Need a mirror? It's in your hand. Need a copy of your favorite book? Now it's in your hand. Would you like to nap? A nap-pod would be delivered to your door in minutes.

The galactic information networks were sending remote-controlled camera-crew robots. In moments, they would fill the school auditorium. Benzo's programming class, including Plexi, was asked to come along. They would be the background. Benzo was more of a "foreground person," he said. Eye-bots from all the major information networks hummed and hovered throughout the auditorium. A voice asked him to explain his app to the galaxy's people.

"My app is called the Encouragement Patch," announced Benzo. "It includes the latest human psychology programming. It finds a way to encourage you to do the right things. The idea is that it just won't take no for an answer!"

For a while, the Encouragement Patch did **pique** people's interest. They were curious because it was new. People tried it and listened to their E.T. People lost weight and learned foreign languages. Kids finished their homework without any parents asking them. People ate healthy food. Everybody got paperwork done on time. For a while, the Encouragement Patch app was more popular than oxygen!

However, by springtime, people everywhere were complaining that the Encouragement Patch was driving them crazy. No matter how many excuses they gave the E.T., it kept nagging them. So Benzo and Plexi began working on a new idea. It was called the Courage Patch. It gave people the courage to stand up to their E.T. and tell it who was really boss. It sold very fast.

App of the Year

Plexi's best friend, Benzo, won the galaxy's biggest prize: the App of the Year. Benzo's app was chosen to be a part of the E.T., or Everything Tech. All people lived with the E.T. from the time they were born.

The E.T. could do everything! The E.T. was your phone. It showed a hologram, or three-dimensional image, of the person you were talking to. The E.T. was your link to the Information Cloud. The Information Cloud could find out anything you wanted to know. The E.T. could not only do anything, but it could be anything. If you need a mirror, then a mirror appears in your hand. If you need a copy of your favorite book, then it appears in your hand. If you would like to nap, a nap-pod is delivered to your door in minutes.

The galactic information networks were busy. They sent remote-control camera-crew robots. In moments, they would fill the school auditorium. Benzo's programming class, including Plexi, was asked to come along. They would be the background. Benzo was more of a "foreground person," he said. Eye-bots from all the major information networks hummed and hovered throughout the auditorium. A voice asked him to explain his app to the galaxy's people.

"My app is called the Encouragement Patch," announced Benzo. "It includes the latest human psychology programming. It finds a way to encourage you to do the right things. The idea is that it just won't take no for an answer!"

For a while, the Encouragement Patch did pique people's interest. They were curious because it was new. People tried it and listened to their E.T. People lost weight and learned foreign languages. Kids finished their homework without any parents asking them. People ate healthy food. Everybody got paperwork done on time. For a while, the Encouragement Patch app was more popular than oxygen!

However, by springtime, people everywhere were complaining that the Encouragement Patch was driving them crazy. No matter how many excuses they gave the E.T., it kept nagging them. So Benzo and Plexi began working on a new idea. It was called the Courage Patch. It gave people the courage to stand up to their E.T. It sold very fast.

App of the Year

It was the biggest thing that ever happened at Plexi's middle school, Andromeda Central. Plexi's best friend, Benzo, won the galaxy's biggest prize: the App of the Year. This was the application chosen to be added to the E.T., or Everything Tech, that people lived with from birth.

The E.T. could do, well, everything. It was your phone, projecting a hologram of the person you were talking to. It was your link to the Information Cloud, so it could find out literally anything you wanted to know. The E.T. could not only do anything, but it could be anything. Need a mirror? It's in your hand. Need a copy of *From the Mixed-Up Files of Mrs. Basil E. Frankweiler*? It's where your mirror used to be. Would you like a nap? *Voilà!* A nap-pod with a cozy bed there in minutes flat.

The galactic information networks were sending remote-controlled camera-crew robots at this very moment to the school auditorium. Benzo's whole programming class, including Plexi, was asked to come along to provide background. Benzo was more of a "foreground person," he said. Eye-bots from all the major information networks hummed and hovered throughout the auditorium. A voice out of nowhere asked Benzo to explain his app to the galaxy's people.

"My app," Benzo announced, "which I call the Encouragement Patch, includes the latest human psychology programming and an engine that finds a way to encourage you to do the right things. In fact, the whole idea is that it just won't take no for an answer!"

For a while, because it was new, the Encouragement Patch did pique people's interest. People tried it and listened to their E.T. People lost weight and learned foreign languages. Kids finished their homework without any parents nagging them. Sales of healthy food skyrocketed. At its peak, the Encouragement Patch app was more popular than oxygen!

However, by springtime, people from every inhabited planet were complaining that the Encouragement Patch was driving them crazy. No matter how many excuses they gave the E.T., it kept nagging them. So Benzo and Plexi began working on a new idea: It was called the Courage Patch. It gave people the power to stand up to their E.T. Encouragement Patch and tell it who was really boss. It sold like hotcakes.

Name _____ Date _____

Use what you read in the passage to answer the questions.

1. What does Benzo win?

_____

_____

2. What do all people have from the time they're born?

_____

_____

3. How do people get information from their E.T.?

_____

_____

4. The galactic information networks of the future are like what in our time?

_____

_____

5. Why does the programming class go to the auditorium?

_____

_____

6. What does the Encouragement Patch do?

_____

_____

7. What does **pique** mean? What is something that piques your interest?

_____

_____

8. What causes Benzo and Plexi to work on the Courage Patch?

_____

_____

Overview II: Introduction to
Informational Text

What Is It?

What is informational text?

Nonfiction text is an important tool for learning. Informational text informs about Social Studies or Science topics. Factual text increases our knowledge of the world.

Examples

What are some examples of informational text?

- Brochures and pamphlets
- Encyclopedia entries
- Magazine articles
- Online reference articles
- Reference books
- Textbooks

Purpose

What is the purpose of reading informational text?

Informational text helps us learn information and explore different thoughts and issues. It also helps prepare the brain for more difficult information and prepare for real-life reading as an adult.

Audience

Who is the audience for informational text?

Informational text serves to educate the reader on a topic. Some readers prefer reading nonfiction to fiction. They would rather get information they can use or that makes them smarter, instead of reading imagined stories.

How to Use It

How do you read informational text?

1. Think about what you already know about the topic.
2. Think about what you would like to know.
3. Ask yourself what you learned.

What are some common features of informational text?

Usually includes boldfaced words or some other special text treatment to highlight words and key concepts

Has an author who has knowledge of the topic

Includes photos or realistic drawings

Informational Text

Is factual and backed up by research or expert opinions

Has headings and subheadings

May have a table of contents, glossary, appendix, and/or index

Often has charts, graphs, maps, tables, time lines, labels, captions, and/or diagrams

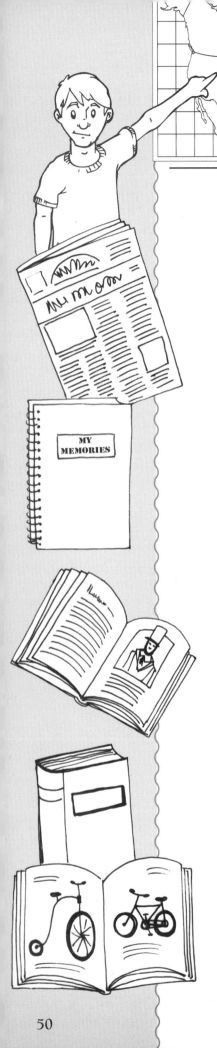

Social Studies

Why do we study Social Studies?

In Social Studies, we learn about the people in our world and how they relate to one another. We learn how they live, manage their communities, and relate to other groups. We also learn their values and what they seek to accomplish.

Why do we study early explorers?

The early explorers ventured by land and sea to find new trading partners, new goods, and new routes for trade. They also were curious about other peoples and other lands. Their explorations improved our knowledge of geography through extensive mapping and storytelling.

Why do we study the American Revolution?

Understanding what happened during the American Revolution helps us appreciate the issues and struggles that lead to war. When we study the American Revolution, we appreciate the sacrifices that were made for the freedoms that some people may take for granted.

Why do we study the U.S. Constitution?

The U.S. Constitution is one of the most influential documents of all time. Not only is it the supreme law of the United States, but it has been used as a model document in over 200 countries! The Constitution is a living document, and therefore it is reviewed and argued regularly for possible changes, or amendments.

Why do we study the Civil War?

We should study the Civil War to appreciate how people struggled to create the America that we know today. The Civil War brought an end to slavery and paved the way for greater civil rights for all Americans, no matter their race or religion. The Civil War also united the North and the South into one country.

Shows how people manage themselves and work together as a society

Compares people's similarities and differences

Shows how different peoples live their lives

Tells about people and groups of people

Social Studies Text

Shows how governments are run

Helps teach us how to participate as citizens in a society

Encourages us to make judgments about issues

Early Explorers

Spanish explorers came to Mexico in 1517. They saw people wearing gold. They wanted the gold. Spain sent Hernán Cortés to Mexico to find gold. Cortés was a conquistador. A conquistador is a conqueror.

In February 1519, Cortés sailed to Mexico. He took 600 men, fifteen horses, and eleven ships. The Spanish fought villagers. They used guns and swords. The villagers only had spears and arrows. Cortés wanted to find the emperor of the Aztec Empire. His name was Montezuma. He lived in the capital. The capital was Tenochtitlán.

In April, Cortés landed in the Aztec Empire. The empire was big. Cortés burned his own ships because he did not want his men to leave. He wanted them to stay and fight the Aztecs. The Aztecs were strong fighters. They were good builders, too. The Aztecs knew about math and astronomy. Astronomy is the study of the skies. The Aztecs prayed to a sun god. They killed their enemies for the sun god.

Montezuma sent gifts of gold to Cortés. Montezuma hoped Cortés would take the gold and leave. But Cortés didn't leave.

Cortés and his men began a long march to the capital. Some natives joined Cortés. They did not like the Aztec rulers. The rulers were cruel. Cortés got to the capital. Montezuma welcomed him. He gave Cortés more gifts. Montezuma treated Cortés's men like kings.

The capital city was amazing to Cortés. It was on an island in the middle of a lake. There were temples, palaces, and pyramids. More than 200,000 people lived in the capital.

Cortés took control of the city. He put Montezuma in jail. He took Montezuma's gold and silver.

The Aztecs fought back. They chased the Spanish out of the city. Montezuma died in the battle. Cortés came back a year later. This time the Spanish won. The capital was destroyed. The Aztec Empire came to an end. Cortés built Mexico City where the Aztec capital had been.

Early Explorers

Early explorers had reached Mexico in 1517. There they had seen people wearing gold. Hernán Cortés was a conquistador. Cortés wanted to find the gold. In February of 1519, Cortés set sail with 600 men, fifteen horses, and eleven ships. The villagers fought with bows and arrows. Cortés and his men had guns and swords. The villagers had no chance to win.

In April, Cortés reached the city of Veracruz. Now he was in the Aztec Empire. This was the place he had been looking for. Cortés burned his ships because he did not want any of his men to go back to Cuba. Cortés wanted to fight and defeat the Aztecs.

The Aztec Empire was big. It stretched across central Mexico. The Aztecs were skilled fighters. They were also good builders. The Aztecs knew about math and astronomy, the study of the skies. They worshipped a sun god. The Aztecs killed their enemies to honor the sun god.

Montezuma ruled the Aztecs. Montezuma lived in the capital, Tenochtitlán. When Cortés arrived in Veracruz, Montezuma sent him huge gifts of gold. Montezuma hoped Cortés would take the gold and leave. Cortés did not leave. Cortés wanted to take over the capital.

Cortés began a long march to the capital. Along the way, some of the native people joined his army. They did not like the Aztec rulers. They were tired of paying high taxes. Cortés reached the capital. Montezuma welcomed him. Montezuma gave Cortés more gifts. Montezuma treated Cortés like a king.

The capital was an amazing city. It was built on an island in the middle of a large lake. It had temples, palaces, and pyramids. More than 200,000 people lived in the capital. Cortés took control of the city. He put Montezuma in jail. Cortés melted down the ruler's gold and silver. He turned the gold and silver into bars and took it back to Spain.

The Aztecs fought back. They chased the Spanish out of the city, but Montezuma died in the battle. Cortés came back a year later. This time the Spanish defeated the Aztecs. The Aztec Empire ended. Cortés built Mexico City on the same site as the Aztec capital.

Early Explorers

In 1517, Spanish explorers reached the coast of Mexico and saw people wearing hammered gold jewelry and precious jewels. The rulers of Spain wanted gold, so they sent the conquistador Hernán Cortés to Mexico to find it.

In February of 1519, Cortés set sail with 600 men and fifteen horses in eleven ships. They landed on the mainland of Mexico. Cortés and his men attacked the Native American villagers. The villagers didn't stand a chance with their spears and arrows. The Spanish had swords and guns.

In April, Cortés landed at a spot he named Veracruz. Now he was in the land of Montezuma, the emperor of the Aztec Empire. The Aztec Empire stretched across central Mexico. The Aztecs were skilled warriors and talented builders. They knew about math and astronomy, the study of the skies. They worshipped a sun god and sacrificed, or killed, their enemies to honor him.

In Tenochtitlán, the Aztec capital, Montezuma was told of the Spaniards' arrival. He sent messengers to Veracruz with huge gifts of gold for Cortés. The Aztec emperor hoped that Cortés would take the gold and leave. But, Cortés became more determined to reach Tenochtitlán.

Cortés began a long march toward the capital. The Spaniards passed through areas where different tribes lived. Many became Cortés's allies, or friends. The Aztecs had many enemies because they were such harsh rulers. When Cortés reached the capital, he was amazed. The city was built on an island in the middle of a huge lake. It had temples, palaces, and towering pyramids. Tenochtitlán was home to more than 200,000 people.

Cortés put Montezuma in jail and took control of the city. He melted down the ruler's gold and silver, turning it into bars to bring back to Spain. Eventually, the Aztecs rebelled and chased the Spaniards out. Montezuma died in the rebellion. Determined not to give up, Cortés returned a year later with more troops, both Spanish and Native American. The fighting was fierce, but the Spaniards and their allies won. The Aztec Empire was finished. From there, the Spanish spread out through Central America.

Name _____ Date _____

Use what you read in the passage to answer the questions.

1. What was Cortés looking for in Mexico?

_____

_____

2. Why were the Spanish able to defeat the villagers easily?

_____

_____

3. Who ruled the Aztecs?

_____

_____

4. What was the name of the city where Montezuma lived?

_____

_____

5. Why did Montezuma give gold to Cortés?

_____

_____

6. Why does the author describe the capital city as "amazing"?

_____

_____

7. How does the author describe the Aztecs?

_____

_____

8. What caused the Aztec Empire to come to an end?

_____

_____

The Stamp Act

In March 1765, the British Stamp Act became a law. The law said that every paper had to have a British stamp. That meant every book, newspaper, and more. Colonists had to pay for the stamps. This payment was called a tax. The tax made the colonists angry. The colonists thought the Stamp Act was unfair. It was unfair because they did not get to vote on it. They did not have representatives in the British government. Representatives are people who speak or act for other people.

Representatives from nine colonies met in October 1765. They made a list of rights. One right was that they get to choose the people who represent them. They also said that only a government they vote for can tax them. They sent the list to the king.

Many colonists fought the Stamp Act. Some did not pay the tax. Others would not buy things from the British. Some burned the stamps. The king ended the Stamp Act in 1766. The colonists were still angry. They didn't like the king's rules.

The king sent 4,000 soldiers to Boston, Massachusetts. The soldiers stopped ships from going in and out of Boston Harbor. Now the colonists couldn't trade, or buy and sell things, with other countries.

On March 5, 1770, a group of angry colonists threw snowballs at British soldiers. A few British soldiers fired into the crowd. Three colonists were killed. Later, two more colonists died. This was the Boston Massacre. Colonists who did not want to obey the king became known as rebels.

The Stamp Act

In March 1765, Britain passed a law called the Stamp Act. The act made colonists pay taxes on every printed piece of paper they used. The colonists had to pay taxes on books and newspapers. The British needed the money from these taxes to pay for wars. The British thought the colonies should help pay for military protection. The colonists said they would not pay. The colonists had no representatives in the British government. They had no vote. They didn't think Britain should tax them without their votes.

In October 1765, representatives from nine colonies met. They sent King George III a list of rights that they wanted. Number Five said: "That the only representatives of the people of these colonies are persons chosen by themselves." The colonists said they could only be taxed by their own elected government, or legislatures.

The colonists joined together to fight against the Stamp Act. Some people refused to buy British goods. Some people did not pay the tax. Other people burned the stamps. The British leaders were very surprised by the colonists' actions. The king put an end to the Stamp Act in 1766. He was not happy. The colonists were out of his control.

In the coming years, things did not get better. People were still not happy. They did not like the king's rules. The king sent 4,000 soldiers to Boston, Massachusetts. The British soldiers enforced the king's rules. They also stopped ships from sailing in and out of Boston Harbor. This stopped the colonists from trading goods with other countries.

On the night of March 5, 1770, a mob grew. Some colonists threw snowballs at British soldiers. A shoving match followed. The night turned deadly. A few British soldiers fired into the crowd. Three colonists were killed. Later, two more colonists died. This event became known as the Boston Massacre. The colonists who did not obey the king became known as rebels.

The Stamp Act

In March 1765, the British government passed a law called the Stamp Act. It forced colonists to pay taxes on any printed item they bought from Britain. This meant books, calendars, playing cards, and many more everyday items would be taxed. The colonists were angry.

The British said the money from taxes would pay for British troops who protected the colonists. But many colonists objected. They had no representatives in the British government. They felt that Britain had no right to force more taxes on them without their vote.

In October 1765, representatives from nine colonies met. They sent King George III a list of thirteen rights they demanded be theirs. Number Five said: "That the only representatives of the people of these colonies are persons chosen by themselves; and that no taxes ever have been or can be constitutionally imposed on them but by their respective legislatures."

Many colonists disagreed with the Stamp Act. They said that they would not buy British goods. Some colonists simply refused to pay the taxes. Others burned stamps or destroyed the building where taxes were collected. These actions did not go unnoticed. By 1766, the king put an end to the Stamp Act.

Even after the Stamp Act ended, many colonists still objected to the king's strict rules. They wouldn't buy British goods. The king sent 4,000 British soldiers to keep order in Boston. The soldiers also kept ships from sailing in and out of Boston Harbor. The colonists could no longer trade goods with other nations.

On the night of March 5, 1770, a mob of colonists threw snowballs at British soldiers. A shoving match followed. Then it turned deadly. A few British soldiers fired their guns into the crowd. By the time the last shot was fired, three colonists lay dead. Later, two more colonists died from their wounds. This event became known as the Boston Massacre. The colonists who did not want to obey the king's rule became known as rebels.

Name _____ Date _____

Use what you read in the passage to answer the questions.

1. When did the British government pass the Stamp Act?

_____

_____

2. What is a tax?

_____

_____

3. How did the colonists feel about the Stamp Act? Why?

_____

_____

4. Why did the colonists care about having representation?

_____

_____

5. In what ways did colonists fight against the Stamp Act?

_____

_____

6. Why did the king end the Stamp Act?

_____

_____

7. Why were ships stopped from going in and out of Boston Harbor?

_____

_____

8. What conclusion can you draw about the Boston Massacre?

_____

_____

No Bill of Rights, No Constitution

The U.S. Constitution was a plan. It said how the new government would work. The government would have three branches. The president would lead the executive branch. This branch would carry out laws. Congress would lead the legislative branch. This branch would make the laws. The Supreme Court would lead the judicial branch. This branch would decide if the laws were fair.

On September 17, 1787, the U.S. Constitution was ready. The Framers met to sign it. The Framers are the men who wrote the plan. But some Framers felt the plan was not complete. They wanted it to include a list of freedoms.

Most of the men were tired. They wanted the Constitution to be signed. Thirty-eight of the delegates signed the document. Three delegates did not. A delegate is a person who represents other people.

All of the states had to approve the Constitution. Many people voted against it. People fought over whether or not to include a list of freedoms. People who did not want a list of freedoms were Federalists. Federalists wanted a strong central government. They wanted the central government to share power with the state governments. The people against the Constitution were Anti-Federalists. They were afraid the Constitution would not give the states enough power. They thought the national government might take away the rights of the states.

For the Constitution to become law, nine states had to ratify it. To win votes, the Federalists made a promise. If the states approved the Constitution, the Federalists would make sure the Constitution included a bill of rights.

The promise worked. The states ratified the Constitution. George Washington became the nation's first president. He took office on April 30, 1789. Two months later, James Madison presented seventeen amendments to the Constitution to Congress. Amendments are changes. The amendments promised certain rights and freedoms.

No Bill of Rights, No Constitution

On September 17, 1787, the U.S. Constitution was ready. The Constitution was a six-page plan for a new government. The government would have three branches.

The president would lead the executive branch. This branch would carry out laws. Congress would lead the legislative branch. This branch would make the laws. The Supreme Court would lead the judicial branch. This branch would decide if the laws were fair.

The plan was brilliant, and the Framers, the men who wrote the plan, gathered to sign it. But some Framers felt the plan was incomplete and wanted the plan to contain a list of freedoms.

Most of the men were tired, and they wanted the Constitution to be signed. Thirty-eight of the delegates signed the document, but three delegates did not. Then the thirteen states had to ratify, or approve, the plan. Many people voted against the Constitution, because they wanted it to have a bill of rights. In the end, the Constitution was approved. But many people still wanted it to contain a bill of rights.

The public fought over a bill of rights. Some people did not want a bill of rights. These people were called Federalists. They wanted a federal system. They wanted a strong central government that shared power with the state governments. The people against the Constitution were called Anti-Federalists. They were afraid the Constitution made the states too weak. They thought the central government might take away the rights of the states.

Nine states had to ratify the Constitution before it became law. To win votes, the Federalists made a promise. If the states ratified the Constitution, the Federalists would amend it. They would make sure the Constitution had a list of rights that no government could take away.

The promise worked, and the states ratified the Constitution. George Washington became the nation's first president, and he took office on April 30, 1789. Two months later, James Madison presented seventeen amendments to Congress.

No Bill of Rights, No Constitution

On September 17, 1787, most of the men who wrote the U.S. Constitution gathered to sign it. They had created a six-page plan for a new form of government. The plan described the duties of three branches of government. The executive branch would carry out laws. The legislative branch would pass laws. The judicial branch would form a system of national courts. The plan was brilliant.

However, at least three of the Framers, the men who wrote the Constitution, felt it wasn't complete. They wanted the Constitution to contain a bill of rights, or list of freedoms.

Most of the delegates were tired. They wanted the Constitution to be signed. Therefore, thirty-eight of the delegates, including George Washington, signed the document. The three delegates who wanted a bill of rights did not. People in the thirteen states then had to ratify, or approve, the Constitution. Many people voted against the Constitution because it did not have a bill of rights. In the end, the Constitution was approved, but it was clear that a bill of rights was needed.

The fight over a bill of rights went public as soon as newspapers published the Constitution. People in favor of the Constitution without a bill of rights called themselves Federalists. They wanted a federal system, a type of government in which power is shared by national and state governments.

The people against the Constitution were called Anti-Federalists. They liked the idea of a federal system, but they thought the Constitution made the states too weak. They were also concerned that the national government might be powerful enough to take away the rights of the states.

To win the votes of Anti-Federalists, the Federalists made a promise. If the states ratified the Constitution, the Federalists would work hard to get it amended. They would make sure the Constitution contained a list of rights that no government could take away. The promise satisfied many Anti-Federalists. The states ratified the Constitution. The nation's first president, George Washington, took office on April 30, 1789. Two months later, Congressman James Madison presented seventeen constitutional amendments to the U.S. Congress.

●●●

Name _____ Date _____

Use what you read in the passage to answer the questions.

1. What is the U.S. Constitution?

_____

_____

2. What are the three branches of the U.S. government?

_____

_____

3. Which branch makes sure laws are obeyed?

_____

_____

4. Why didn't three of the men sign the Constitution on September 17, 1787?

_____

_____

5. What did Federalists and Anti-Federalists disagree about?

_____

_____

6. How did the Federalists win votes?

_____

_____

7. How can you tell that the Federalists' promise worked?

_____

_____

8. What are amendments? Why are they important to the Constitution?

_____

_____

Underground Railroad

The Underground Railroad was not a real railroad. It was a secret group. The people in the group wanted to abolish slavery. **Abolish** means to end. People could be killed for helping slaves. But they did it anyway. They helped slaves run away. The Underground Railroad began in the 1830s. The slaves stayed in safe houses. Safe houses were safe places for slaves to sleep and eat. The Underground Railroad led slaves to free states in the North. Many people living in Northern states took care of slaves.

Workers on the Underground Railroad talked in secret code. They used railroad words for the secret words. The slaves were called "parcels." **Parcels** means packages. A "conductor" took the slaves to "stations." But the stations were really safe houses. Some "stations" had rooms behind fake walls. Others had secret passages. These helped slaves get away quickly. A safe house owner was called a "stationmaster." The slaves got hot meals at the safe house. The stationmaster passed messages to other helpers. They took slaves in wagons to the next station. They gave the slaves shoes and clothes. These clothes helped the slaves look like free people.

There were at least 3,000 people working the Underground Railroad. Most of them worked in secret. They did not want people who were catching slaves to find out. It was dangerous to help slaves. Angry slave owners attacked some helpers. Others had helpers arrested. Most helpers worked in the free states. Some brave helpers worked near the Ohio River. The Ohio River was between a slave state and a free state. Kentucky was a slave state. Ohio was a free state. Many slaves were led to cities on the Great Lakes. Slaves could take special boats to Canada. Slavery was against the law in Canada.

A Slave Law was passed in 1850 in the U.S. The law let people catch slaves and take them back to their "owners." As a result, thousands of slaves went to Canada to hide.

Underground Railroad

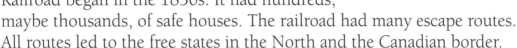

The Underground Railroad was not a real railroad. It was a secret group of people. These people wanted to abolish, or end, slavery. They were called abolitionists. Some members were free black people. Some members were former slaves. Other members were white people. They all risked their lives to help slaves escape. They helped fugitives, or runaway slaves, travel many miles. The Underground Railroad began in the 1830s. It had hundreds, maybe thousands, of safe houses. The railroad had many escape routes. All routes led to the free states in the North and the Canadian border.

People who worked for the Underground Railroad were called "agents." Agents sent messages in code. They used railroad terms. Runaway slaves were "parcels," or packages. A "conductor" took "passengers" to "stations," or safe houses. Slaves hid in attics and cellars. Some stations had rooms behind fake walls. Other homes had secret passages. Fugitives could escape quickly. A safe house owner was a "stationmaster." They gave the runaways food and comfort. Runaways were scared, cold, and tired. At the station, they found hot meals and blankets. The stationmaster passed messages between conductors and sent information to other stations. Friends might help by lending wagons to carry slaves to the next station. Local men donated shoes and suits. Women sewed shirts and dresses. With new clothes, runaway slaves looked like free people. That made escape easier.

At least 3,000 people were Underground Railroad agents. Most worked in secret. They did not want records to fall into the hands of slave catchers. It was dangerous to be an agent. Angry slave owners attacked some agents. Others had agents arrested. Most agents worked in the free states. Some brave agents worked in the "borderland." This was the land along the Ohio River. The river formed the northern border of Kentucky. Kentucky was a slave state. Conductors met slaves at night. Then they took the slaves across the river to the free state of Ohio. Many routes led to port cities on the Great Lakes. From there, fugitives could take "abolition boats" to Canada. Slavery was illegal in Canada.

In 1850, the Fugitive Slave Law was passed. The law let slave catchers bring fugitives in free states back to slave states. As a result, thousands of fugitives went to Canada.

Underground Railroad

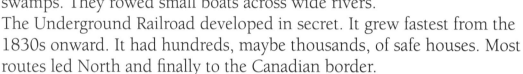

The Underground Railroad was not a real railroad. It was a series of routes and safe houses used by escaping slaves. The Underground Railroad also referred to the people who helped the slaves. These people were made up of free black people, former slaves, and white people. They wanted to abolish slavery. So they risked their safety to help escaping slaves. They led runaways, or fugitives, through dangerous swamps. They rowed small boats across wide rivers. The Underground Railroad developed in secret. It grew fastest from the 1830s onward. It had hundreds, maybe thousands, of safe houses. Most routes led North and finally to the Canadian border.

Workers, or "agents," on the Underground Railroad sent messages in code using railroad terms. Runaway slaves were "packages" or "parcels." A "conductor" took "passengers" to "stations," or safe houses. The slaves hid in attics or cellars until it was safe to move on. Some homes had rooms behind fake walls or sliding panels. Other stations had secret passages. These helped fugitives escape quickly. A safe house owner was the "stationmaster." He and his family did more than hide the fugitives. They gave the runaways food and comfort. At the station, they found hot meals and soft blankets to sleep on. The stationmaster organized a local network. He passed messages between conductors. He sent information to other stations. His neighbors might lend wagons to carry "passengers" to the next station. That made escape easier.

Probably 3,000 or more people were Underground Railroad agents. Most agents worked in secret. They did not want any records to fall into the hands of the slave catchers. It was dangerous to be an agent. Angry slaveholders attacked some agents. Others had agents arrested. Most agents lived and worked in free states. Some brave conductors worked on the northern border of the slave state of Kentucky. These conductors met fugitives at night and took them across the Ohio River to the free state of Ohio. Many routes led to port cities on the Great Lakes. From those ports, fugitives could travel to Canada on "abolition boats."

In 1850, the Fugitive Slave Law was passed in the United States. The law allowed slave catchers to take fugitives from free states to their owners in slave states. As a result, thousands of fugitives went to Canada where slavery was illegal.

●●●

Name _____ Date _____

Use what you read in the passage to answer the questions.

1. Whom did the Underground Railroad help?

_____

_____

2. What does **abolish** mean?

_____

_____

3. Why was it dangerous to be a helper or "agent" on the Underground Railroad?

_____

_____

4. What is a "parcel" on the Underground Railroad?

_____

_____

5. Where did the Underground Railroad go?

_____

_____

6. What was the difference between a "conductor" and a "stationmaster"?

_____

_____

7. Why might a station have a fake wall or secret passageway?

_____

_____

8. Why might a runaway slave choose to go to Canada rather than a Northern state?

_____

_____

Unit 6 Mini-Lesson
Science

Why do we study Science?

Science helps us understand the world around us. To participate in society, you must know some science. As examples, to cook dinner means you understand hot and cold, chemical reactions, and the effects of combinations of ingredients. When you ride a roller coaster, you understand that centrifugal force will keep you in your seat. To vote for a candidate, a person weighs environmental threats with costs. When you choose to eat an apple rather than a bag of chips, you have considered your nutrition. When you choose not to smoke, you are choosing the health of your lungs over peer pressure. All these decisions involve science understanding.

Why do we study life science?

Earth is full of life, and life science studies the living things on Earth. Life science studies animals and plants and the environments and habitats where they live. Life science studies how living things meet their needs for water and food. And it studies the life cycles of living things—how they grow and change over time.

Why do we study physical science?

Physical science involves the study of nonliving things in our world. When you use a fan to cool yourself off, when you use a computer to send an e-mail, when you mix vinegar and water to clean windows, or when you use a magnet to pick up a tack, you are employing physical science. Physical science study in school often includes laboratory work, such as experiments.

Why do we study earth science?

Earth science is the study of Earth as well as things in outer space. Builders use earth science to protect their buildings against high winds and earthquakes. Fishermen use earth science to know the best times to fish, the best places for fishing, and which fish they should keep to be responsible stewards of the sea. As adults, one must make decisions to prevent pollution, use energy responsibly, ration resources, and more. Everyone needs to understand some earth science in order to be a caretaker of our planet.

Unit 6 • Common Core Comprehension Grade 5 • ©2012 Newmark Learning, LLC

Contains factual information about our planet and its neighbors in space

Studies how life forms change over time

Shows how different plants and animals live

Tells about the differences in living and nonliving things

Science Text

Inspires us to think like a scientist

Includes special text features, such as photos, labels, captions, diagrams, and sidebars

Explains scientific terms

Encourages good decisions about protecting and preserving the environment

Skeletal System

Your skull is at the top of your spine. Your skull is your head bone. The spine is a group of bones. It holds up your head. It supports your skeleton. The spine lets you bend, twist, and turn your body. The spine is also called the spinal column. The spine also connects your skull to your pelvis and legs.

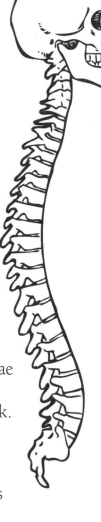

The cranium is the part of the skull that covers your brain. The cranium is very hard. It protects your brain if you get hit in the head. The cranium is very strong, but it can still be hurt. You must take care of it. Always wear a helmet when you skateboard, ride your bike, or play football.

Your bottom jaw is connected to the cranium in front of your ears. The bottom jaw is called the mandible. The mandible moves. It holds your teeth. The cranium and the mandible make up the skull.

The bones in your spinal column are called vertebrae. Vertebrae are stacked on top of one another, like building blocks. Between each vertebrae bone is a soft cushion. This cushion is called a disk. The disks stop the vertebrae from rubbing together.

Disks are made of cartilage. Cartilage is smooth and slippery. It covers the ends of bones and joints. Joints are where two bones meet. Your ears and nose are made of cartilage, too.

The spinal cord goes through the center of the spine. The spinal cord is your body's main nerve. It connects the brain to the rest of the body. Inside the spinal cord is a liquid. The liquid is called spinal fluid. Spinal fluid protects the cord from being hurt.

Skeletal System

The skull sits on top of the spinal column. The spinal column supports the entire skeleton. The spinal column connects your skull to your pelvis and legs. The part of the skull that covers the brain is the cranium. The cranium is a very hard shell. This shell protects the brain in case you hit your head on a hard surface.

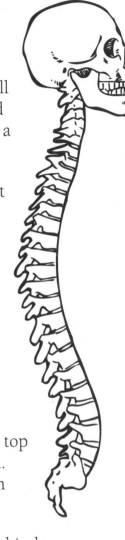

The cranium is very strong, but it can still be hurt. You must take care of it. Always wear a helmet when you skateboard, ride your bike, or play football. The lower jaw connects to the cranium in front of the ears. This is called the mandible. The mandible moves, and it holds the teeth. Together, the cranium and the mandible form the skull.

The spinal column holds your head up. The spinal column supports your chest. It also lets you bend, twist, and turn your body.

The spinal column is a group of bones called vertebrae. Vertebrae fit together like building blocks. They are stacked on top of one another. In between each two vertebrae is a soft cushion. This cushion is called a disk. The disks keep the vertebrae from rubbing together.

Disks are made of cartilage. Cartilage is connective tissue. It binds, or holds, other tissues together. Cartilage is smooth and slippery. It covers the ends of bones and joints. It also forms the ears and nose.

The spinal cord runs through the center of the spinal column. The spinal cord is the body's main nerve. It connects the brain to the rest of the body. The spinal cord lies in the spinal canal. The spinal canal is filled with a liquid called spinal fluid. The spinal fluid protects the cord from being harmed.

Skeletal System

The skull sits on top of and attaches to the spinal column. The spinal column supports the entire skeleton. It not only supports, but it allows you to bend, twist, and turn your body. The major part of the skull (the part that covers the brain) is the cranium. The cranium covers the brain with a very hard shell. This shell is necessary to prevent damage to the brain. It protects your head in case you hit it on a hard surface.

The cranium is very strong, but it can still be damaged. So you must protect it. Always wear a helmet when you skateboard, ride your bike, or play football. If you look closely at the skull, you will see that the lower jaw is connected to the cranium just in front of the ears. The lower jaw is called the mandible. It moves and contains teeth. Together, the cranium, the mandible, and other facial bones form the skull.

The spinal column is the major support structure of the skeleton. It holds the head up and supports the chest. It also attaches to the pelvis.

The spinal column is actually a group of bones called vertebrae. Vertebrae are individual connected bones that fit together like building blocks. Vertebrae are stacked on top of each other. Between the vertebrae is a tough material called a disk. The disks act like shock absorbers. They keep the vertebrae from rubbing together, and allow the back to move.

Disks are made of cartilage. Cartilage is a kind of tissue called connective tissue. It is called connective tissue because it holds tissues together. Cartilage is spongy, smooth, and flexible. It covers bone ends and joints. It is also the type of support tissue that makes up the ears and nose.

Through the center and along the entire length of the spinal column is the spinal cord. The cord is in the spinal canal. The spinal cord is the main nerve that connects the brain to the rest of the body.

The entire spinal cord is bathed in a clear fluid called spinal fluid. Spinal fluid surrounds the spinal cord and protects it from damage by the disks.

●●●

Name _____ Date _____

Use what you read in the passage to answer the questions.

1. What holds up your head and lets you bend and twist?

_____

_____

2. What is the part of the skull that protects the brain?

_____

_____

3. What is one way you can protect your cranium?

_____

_____

4. What is the mandible?

_____

_____

5. How are vertebrae like building blocks?

_____

_____

6. What would happen if there were no disks in your vertebrae?

_____

_____

7. What parts of your body are made of cartilage?

_____

_____

8. What does spinal fluid do?

_____

_____

Physical Changes

Making a salad is easy. First, you wash the lettuce. Then you chop it. Next, you cut the tomatoes. You peel and slice cucumbers. You put all the vegetables in a bowl. Now you mix them. Finally, you eat the salad. The lettuce is still lettuce. The tomato is still tomato. Each vegetable is still the same type of matter. Matter is anything that has mass and takes up space. Mass is how heavy something is.

When you chop each vegetable, you change that vegetable's shape and size. Shape and size are physical properties. The vegetable looks different, but it is still the same vegetable. It has gone through a physical change.

Changing the shape or size of matter is one kind of physical change. But there are other ways to make physical changes. One way is to add heat to something. Do you ever make marshmallow rice treats? First, you put marshmallows into a pan. Then you turn on the heat on the stove. The marshmallows melt.

All matter is made of tiny parts. The tiny parts are called molecules. Heat makes molecules move faster. The molecules in the marshmallows move faster. This makes the marshmallows melt. The marshmallows become a liquid. The marshmallows are still marshmallows. The heat made a physical change.

PhhhWEEEEEE . . . What is that whistling noise? The water in the teapot is boiling. Heat changes the water into water vapor. Water vapor is a gas. You can't see it. You can't pour this gas into a glass. But it is the same matter as the water you drink.

Melting and boiling are physical changes. Both happen when you add heat. What happens when you take away heat? Fill an ice-cube tray with water. Put it in the freezer. The cold air makes the water molecules move slower. The water freezes. The water is now ice.

Cold can also change a gas to a liquid. First, water vapor meets cold air. Then the vapor loses heat. The molecules slow down. The water vapor condenses. Steam has tiny drops of water. The drops tell you that a physical change happened.

Physical Changes

Do you ever make salad? You probably wash and chop the lettuce, cut the tomatoes, and slice cucumbers. You put all the vegetables in a bowl. Then you mix them all up and add dressing. Now take a bite. The lettuce is still lettuce. The tomato is still a tomato. Each ingredient is still the same type of matter. Matter is anything that has mass and takes up space.

Chopping food changes the shape and size of each type of food. You change a physical property, or characteristic, of the matter. A physical change happens and the matter looks different. But it is still the same type of matter.

You can change the shape or size of matter. For example, you can add heat. Do you ever make crispy rice treats? You melt marshmallows in a pot on low heat. The melted marshmallows are still marshmallows. All matter is made of tiny parts called molecules. Heat makes molecules move faster. As the molecules in a solid move faster, the solid turns into a liquid. The heat caused a physical change.

PhhhWEEEEEE . . . What is that whistling noise? The water in the kettle is boiling. Heat changes the liquid water into a gas. This gas is called water vapor. You cannot pour this gas into a glass. It is the same matter as the water you drink, but in a different form.

Melting and boiling are physical changes. Both happen when you add heat. What happens when you take away heat? Fill an ice-cube tray with water. Put it in the freezer. The cold air makes the water molecules move slower. The liquid freezes. Freezing changes a liquid to a solid. The water is now ice.

Cold can change a gas to a liquid, too. When water vapor meets cold air, the vapor loses heat. The gas molecules slow down. The water vapor condenses, and the gas changes into a liquid. Steam has tiny drops of liquid water. The drops tell you that a physical change happened.

Physical Changes

Do you ever make salad? You might chop lettuce, cut tomatoes, or slice cucumbers. With each bite, you can still taste the lettuce, tomatoes, cucumbers, and dressing. That's because each ingredient is still the same kind of food. Each ingredient is still the same kind of matter. Matter is anything that has mass and takes up space. It is made up of tiny parts called molecules.

Chopping and slicing changes the shape and size of each kind of food. You change a physical property, or characteristic, of the matter. As a result, a physical change occurs. In a physical change, the appearance or form of matter changes, but it is still the same kind of matter.

Changing the size or shape of matter is one way to change it physically. Another way is to add heat to it. Do you ever help make crispy rice treats? You drop the marshmallows into a pan on the stove. Then you turn on the stove to low heat. After a couple of minutes, the marshmallows begin to melt. That's because they gain heat energy. This added heat causes the marshmallow molecules to move faster. As the molecules begin to slip and slide past one another, the solid marshmallows become a gooey liquid, but it is still marshmallow.

PhhhWEEEEEE . . . The liquid water in the kettle is boiling. It's turning into a gas called water vapor. You cannot pour the vapor into a glass, but it's the same matter as the water you drink.

Melting and boiling are physical changes. Both occur when matter gains heat. But what happens when matter loses heat? Different kinds of physical changes occur. When you fill an ice-cube tray and put it in the freezer, heat moves from the liquid water into the cold air of the freezer. The liquid's molecules move slower and slower. They vibrate slowly in place until they form a rigid pattern. That's when the liquid freezes.

When water vapor meets cooler air, the vapor loses heat energy. The water molecules slow down. The water changes back to tiny drops of liquid. The drops are so tiny that they float in the air as a cloud of steam. You might have seen bigger drops of condensation on the inside lid of a pot of boiling water. The drops let you know that another physical change has occurred.

Name _____ Date _____

Use what you read in the passage to answer the questions.

1. What is matter? Give an example.

_____

_____

2. What kind of changes are melting and boiling?

_____

_____

3. What is all matter made of?

_____

_____

4. What happens to molecules when you heat them up?

_____

_____

5. How can you change water into water vapor?

_____

_____

6. What is water vapor?

_____

_____

7. What effect does taking away heat have on water?

_____

_____

8. Do molecules move more quickly or slowly as they cool?

_____

_____

Hurricanes

A hurricane is a huge storm. Hurricanes have lots of rain and wind. Hurricanes are much bigger than thunderstorms.

Thunderstorm winds	20 miles (32 km) per hour
Hurricane winds	150 miles (241 km) per hour or faster
Thunderstorms	can be 2 square miles (5.2 sq. km) wide
Hurricanes	can be hundreds or thousands of square miles
Thunderstorms	may last an hour
Hurricanes	may last for a week or longer

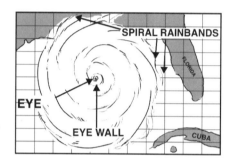

Hurricanes begin over warm ocean water, near the equator. The equator is an imaginary line around the middle of the earth. It is halfway between the North and South poles. Hurricanes can travel for hundreds of miles. Sometimes they hit land. This is called making landfall. Hurricanes happen at certain times of year. Hurricanes last from June to November north of the equator. South of the equator, hurricane season lasts from November to April.

Before a hurricane can begin, two things have to happen. First, the ocean must be at least 80° Fahrenheit (27° Celsius). Oceans get that warm only at certain times of the year. That's why hurricanes have seasons. Second, there needs to be low air pressure. Air pressure is the weight of the air. Air near Earth is always under pressure. The pressure comes from the atmosphere. The atmosphere is the layers of gas that surround Earth. There is high air pressure when the atmosphere pushes down hard on the air. When the atmosphere pushes down less hard, there is low air pressure. When this happens, air can rise more easily.

Meteorologists are scientists who study climate and weather. They use a scale to measure how strong a hurricane is. The scale has five levels. The levels are called categories. The levels are based on wind speed. They are also based on how high the ocean water rises.

A category 3 hurricane or higher can do a lot of damage. The wind can send trees through the air. It can destroy homes. The storm can smash things on the coast. The rain can cause floods and mudslides.

Hurricane Katrina was one of the biggest storms to ever hit the United States. Katrina killed more than 1,000 people. It caused billions of dollars of damage. Most of the damage was in Louisiana, Mississippi, and Florida.

Hurricanes

A hurricane is a huge storm. Hurricanes have heavy rain and strong winds. They are much bigger than thunderstorms. A regular storm has winds of 20 miles (32 kilometers) per hour. A hurricane can have winds of 150 miles (241 kilometers) per hour or more. A regular storm may cover 2 square miles (5.2 square kilometers). A hurricane can cover hundreds or thousands of square miles. A regular storm may last an hour. A hurricane may last for a week or longer.

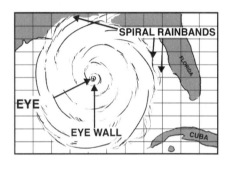

Hurricanes do not happen just anywhere. They begin over warm ocean water near the equator. They can travel for hundreds of miles. Sometimes they hit land. This is called making landfall. Hurricanes come at certain times of year. North of the equator, hurricane season lasts from June to November. South of the equator, hurricane season lasts from November to April.

Hurricanes need two special conditions to form. The first is warm ocean water of at least 80° Fahrenheit (27° Celsius). That is why hurricanes have seasons. Ocean waters get warm enough only at certain times of the year. The second condition is low air pressure.

Air near Earth's surface is always under pressure. The pressure comes from the atmosphere. The atmosphere is the layers of gas that surround Earth. When the atmosphere's weight pushes down with greater force on the surface air, there is high pressure. Sometimes the atmosphere pushes down with less force. Surface air can rise more easily. When this happens, there is low air pressure.

Meteorologists use the Saffir-Simpson scale to measure how strong a hurricane is. The scale has five levels. The levels, or categories, are based on wind speed and how high the ocean water rises.

A hurricane of category 3 or higher can be catastrophic. The wind can hurl trees through the air. It can tear roofs off houses. It can destroy mobile homes. The storm surge can smash things on the coast. The heavy rain can cause floods and mudslides.

Hurricane Katrina was one of the biggest storms ever to hit the United States. Katrina killed more than 1,000 people. It caused billions of dollars of damage. Most of the damage was in Louisiana, Mississippi, and Florida.

Hurricanes

A hurricane is a huge storm with heavy rain and strong winds. It is far more serious than an ordinary thunderstorm. A thunderstorm may cover an area up to 2 square miles (5.2 square kilometers). But a hurricane can cover hundreds or thousands of square miles. A thunderstorm usually lasts for an hour or so. A hurricane may last for a week or longer. An everyday thunderstorm may have winds of 20 miles (32 kilometers) per hour. Yet hurricanes have winds of 150 miles (241 kilometers) per hour.

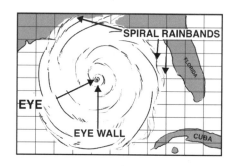

Hurricanes begin over warm ocean water near the equator. They can travel for hundreds of miles, and sometimes they hit land, which is called "making landfall." Hurricanes come at certain times of year. North of the equator, hurricane season lasts from June through November. South of the equator, hurricane season lasts from November through April.

Hurricanes need two special conditions to form. The first requirement is warm ocean water of at least 80° Fahrenheit (27° Celsius). Hurricanes have seasons, because ocean waters get warm enough only at certain times of the year. The second requirement is low air pressure. Air near Earth's surface is always under pressure. The pressure comes from the atmosphere. The atmosphere is the layers of gas that surround Earth. When the atmosphere's weight pushes down with greater force on the surface air, there is high pressure. Sometimes the atmosphere pushes down with less force and surface air can rise more easily. When this happens, there is low air pressure.

Scientists use a scale to measure the intensity, or strength, of a hurricane. The Saffir-Simpson scale has five levels. The levels, or categories, are based on wind speed and storm surge height. A hurricane of category 3 or higher can be truly catastrophic. The winds from a category 3 or higher hurricane can rip trees out of the ground and hurl them through the air. They can tear the roofs off houses. They can destroy mobile homes. Rain causes further damage. The ground can become soaked with more water than it can hold. Whole areas are flooded. Mudslides roar down from the sides of hills.

Hurricane Katrina was one of the biggest storms ever to hit the United States. Katrina killed more than 1,000 people. It caused billions of dollars of damage. Many cities were devastated by the storm.

Name _____ Date _____

Use what you read in the passage to answer the questions.

1. What is the main idea of the passage?

_____

_____

2. How are a hurricane and thunderstorm different?

_____

_____

3. When is hurricane season north of the equator?

_____

_____

4. What two things have to happen for a hurricane to form?

_____

_____

5. What are the layers of gas that surround Earth called?

_____

_____

6. What causes air to rise more easily?

_____

_____

7. What effects might a category 3 hurricane cause?

_____

_____

8. How can you tell that Hurricane Katrina was a very strong storm?

_____

_____

Rocks and Minerals

Gold is a mineral. A mineral is found in rocks and in the ground. Earth has many minerals. Silver and iron are minerals. What makes gold different? Gold has properties that make it different. A property is something you can measure or see. All things have properties. Color and weight are properties. How much something can bend is a property. Being shiny is a property.

Gold's yellow color is a physical property. A physical property is something you can see or measure. You can see the color of gold. The symbol for gold is Au. The symbol comes from the Latin word *aurum*. *Aurum* means "shining dawn." People compare gold's yellow color to the sun. Gold has a bright luster. Luster means shine. Gold is also malleable. Something malleable can be bent easily. Gold is soft. Gold is easy to hammer or press into different shapes. People use gold to make jewelry.

Gold also has chemical properties. Chemical properties change what something is like. Gold is an element. An element is a material that cannot be made into a simpler material. Gold is a stable element. A stable element does not mix easily with other elements, like oxygen. Gold does not corrode. Corrode means to wear away. Some elements rust. Iron is an element that rusts. Gold does not rust. Water or oxygen cannot change gold. Gold can last for years at the bottom of the sea. Gold also stays shiny.

Tiny bits of gold are everywhere. Gold is in almost all rocks and soil. Even seawater has some gold in it. But that gold is not easy to take out. Most gold is found in Earth's crust. The crust is Earth's rocky outer layer. The crust is the ground you walk on. It is the mountains, the river bottoms, and the ocean floor.

Gold is beautiful. Gold is worth a lot. Did you know that gold is also very useful? You can find gold inside a cell phone or computer. What is gold doing there? Most metals are ductile. **Ductile** means you can make the metal into wire. Gold is the most ductile metal on Earth. All metals carry electricity. After copper and silver, gold is the best metal at carrying electricity. Your computer or cell phone has many tiny electronic parts. Each part does a different job. For your machine to work, the parts need to connect. Gold wires often make those connections.

Rocks and Minerals

Gold is a mineral. Minerals are solid materials found in rocks. Earth has many minerals, such as silver and iron. What makes gold different? Gold has certain properties. A property is something that can be measured or seen, such as color and weight. How much something can bend is a property. Being shiny or dull is a property.

Gold's yellow color is a physical property, because you can see the color. The symbol for gold is Au. The symbol comes from the Latin word *aurum*, which means "shining dawn." People compare gold's yellow color to the sun. Gold has a bright luster, or shine. Gold is also malleable, which means it is a soft metal. Gold is easy to hammer or press into different shapes. People use gold to make jewelry.

Gold also has chemical properties. Gold is an element. An element is a pure substance. You cannot break it down into anything smaller. Gold is stable. It does not mix easily with other elements. Gold does not corrode, or wear away. Gold does not rust like iron. Gold is not changed by water or oxygen. Gold can last for years at the bottom of the sea. Gold also keeps its shine.

You can find tiny bits of gold everywhere. Gold is in almost all rocks and soil. Even seawater has some gold in it. But that gold is not easy to extract, or take out. Most gold is found in Earth's crust. The crust is Earth's rocky outer layer. The crust is the ground you walk on. It is the mountains, the river bottoms, and the ocean floor.

Gold is beautiful and valuable. Did you know that it is also very useful? You can find gold inside a cell phone or computer. What is gold doing there? Most metals are ductile. That means you can make them into wire. Gold is the most ductile metal on Earth. You can turn 1 troy ounce of gold into 50 miles (80 kilometers) of wire! All metals conduct, or carry, electricity. After copper and silver, gold is the best metal at conducting electricity. Your computer or cell phone has many tiny electronic parts. Each part does a different job. For your machine to work, the parts need to connect. Gold wires often do that job.

Rocks and Minerals

Gold is a mineral. Minerals are naturally occurring solid substances. There are many minerals on Earth. What makes gold different? Gold has certain properties that make it desirable. A property is something that can be measured or observed. Properties include how heavy something is, whether it bends or is brittle, whether it is shiny or dull, and how it reacts with other substances.

One of gold's physical properties is its yellow color. On the periodic table of elements the symbol for gold is Au. The symbol comes from the Latin word *aurum*, which means "shining dawn." Gold has a bright luster, or shine. It is also malleable. It is a soft metal that can easily be hammered or pressed into different shapes. That's why gold is used to make jewelry.

Gold also has chemical properties. Gold is a stable metal, which means it does not readily combine with other elements. An element is a substance from which compounds are made. Gold does not dissolve or corrode. To corrode means to wear away because of chemical action. Gold does not rust like iron. Gold is not affected by water or oxygen in the air. Gold can last for years at the bottom of the ocean.

You can find tiny amounts of gold in almost all rocks and soil. But it is not easy to recover or extract that gold. Most gold is found within Earth's crust. The crust is the planet's rocky outer layer. This layer includes the ground, the mountains, the river bottoms, and the ocean floor.

Gold is not only beautiful and valuable, it is also very useful. Gold is likely to be inside your computer, game console, or cell phone. Gold, like most metals, is ductile. That means you can easily form it into a wire. Gold is the most ductile metal on Earth. You can turn 1 troy ounce of gold into a thin wire that stretches 50 miles (80 kilometers)!

Like all metals, gold conducts, or provides a pathway for, electricity. After copper and silver, gold is the best metal at conducting electricity. Inside your computer or cell phone are several tiny electronic parts. Each part has a separate function. For your machine to work, the parts need to be connected so they can send electric signals to one another. Gold wires are often used to do that job.

●●●

Name _____ Date _____

Use what you read in the passage to answer the questions.

1. What is one physical property of gold?

_____

_____

2. How is gold like silver and iron? How is it different?

_____

_____

3. How can you tell that gold is soft?

_____

_____

4. What makes gold a stable element?

_____

_____

5. Why is gold able to last for years at the bottom of the sea?

_____

_____

6. Where can you find gold in nature?

_____

_____

7. Which two metals are the best for carrying electricity?

_____

_____

8. What does it mean to be **ductile**?

_____

_____

Overview III: Introduction to
Opinion/Argument

What is an argument?

An argument is a form of writing that tries to convince readers to believe or do something. An argument has a strong point of view about an idea or a problem. It includes facts and examples to support an opinion, and it usually suggests a solution.

Examples

What are some examples of opinion/argument text?

- Advertisements
- Book and film reviews
- Editorials
- Essays
- Letters
- Speeches

Purpose

What is the purpose of an argument?

People write an argument to "sway," or change the minds of, their audience. They want readers to see their points of view. They may want readers to change their minds about a problem or issue. They may also want the readers to take action.

Audience

Who is the audience for an argument?

People write arguments to parents, friends, citizens, business leaders, world leaders, and others. Sometimes they are addressing people who share their views. More often, however, the writer is addressing people who have a different opinion or no opinion. A good argument writer knows the audience and what facts and reasons might change the reader's mind.

How to Use It

How do you read an argument?

Ask yourself:
1. *What is this writer's position, or opinion?*
2. *Does the writer support it with facts and good reasons?*
3. *Do I agree with the writer?*

What are some common features of an opinion/argument?

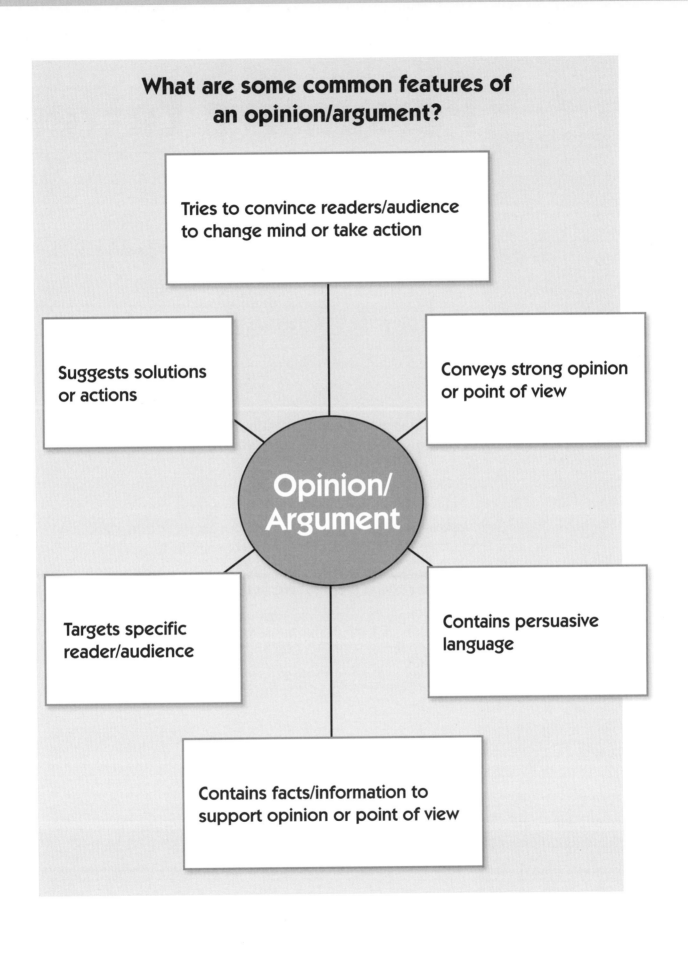

Tries to convince readers/audience to change mind or take action

Suggests solutions or actions

Conveys strong opinion or point of view

Opinion/ Argument

Targets specific reader/audience

Contains persuasive language

Contains facts/information to support opinion or point of view

Persuasive Letters

What is a persuasive letter?

A persuasive letter is a letter that tries to convince readers to believe or do something. A persuasive letter has a strong point of view about an idea or a problem. It includes facts and examples to support an opinion, and it usually suggests a solution.

What is the purpose of a persuasive letter?

People write persuasive letters to "sway," or change the minds of, their readers. They want readers to see their points of view. They may want readers to take action, too.

Who is the audience for a persuasive letter?

People write persuasive letters to all kinds of people: parents, friends, citizens, business leaders, world leaders, and others. They write letters to make people understand their views. They want to change their audience's opinions. For example, a citizen who disagrees with a law might write to a government leader about it. The writer might want the leader to change the law.

How do you read a persuasive letter?

Keep in mind that the writer wants you to support his or her position. Ask yourself: *What is this writer's position, or opinion? Does the writer support it with facts and good reasons? Do I agree with the opinion?* A good persuasive writer knows the audience and what facts and reasons might change the reader's mind.

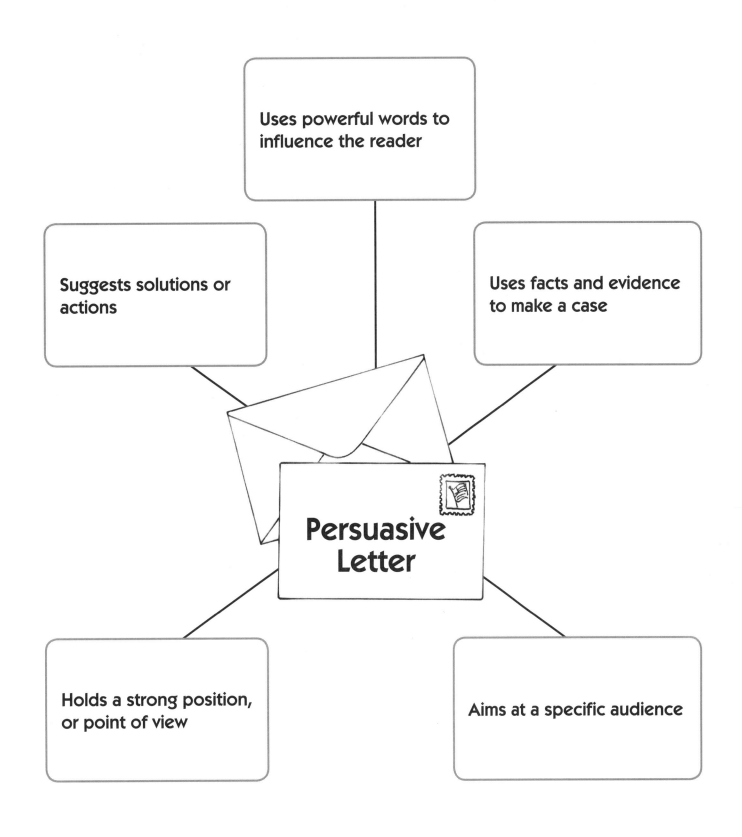

Uses powerful words to influence the reader

Suggests solutions or actions

Uses facts and evidence to make a case

Persuasive Letter

Holds a strong position, or point of view

Aims at a specific audience

Words of a Neutralist: Let Us Live in Peace!

War is very bad. War destroys things. People die in war. Fathers, sons, and brothers die in war. The only way to solve problems is through peaceful talks. We need to each give a little. We need to respect each other's differences. Killing each other will not solve our problems.

Here in Philadelphia, Patriots tell us we must fight England for our freedom. However, the Loyalists tell us the opposite. They say we must fight on England's side. They say we must fight against the Patriots.

The Patriots call this fight an American Revolution. They also call it a War of Independence. The Loyalists call it treason. That means they think we are helping the enemy by not fighting. Some people don't think there should be any government. They are called **anarchists**. Then there are traitors. They go against their own countries. But, no matter what name you give it, it is a fight between people in the same country. It's a civil war. My heart breaks to think about it.

There have been crimes on both sides of this terrible fight. England has made us pay taxes. We did not agree to the taxes. English soldiers have shot at us. The colonists have misbehaved, too. They poured English tea into Boston Harbor. They have put tar and feathers on tax collectors. Both sides are wrong.

There are many of us. We are Quakers, Shakers, Moravians, Mennonites, Amish, and others. We will not fight. We think protecting life is more important than problems with government.

Others believe war goes against what it means to be free. Many people came from England and other countries to the American colonies to escape wars. Some left because they were not allowed to practice their religions. These citizens just wish to be left alone.

We believe war is wicked and unhealthy. No matter what reasons we are given, we will stay neutral. **Neutral** means we will not take a side. We strongly urge you to be neutral, too. We will not send our sons off to take the lives of others! Peace, my friends, at all costs.

—Reverend Nathaniel Thomas

Words of a Neutralist: Let Us Live in Peace!

War is very bad. War destroys things. People die in war. Fathers, sons, and brothers die in war. The only way to solve problems is through peaceful discussion, compromise, and respecting each other's differences. Killing each other will not solve our problems.

Here in Philadelphia, Patriots tell us we must fight England for our freedom. However, the Loyalists tell us the opposite. They say we must fight on England's side. They say we must fight against the Patriots.

The Patriots call this fight an American Revolution or a War of Independence. The Loyalists call it rebellion. The Loyalists say the rebellion is treason led by anarchists and traitors. Treason is helping an enemy during war. Anarchists are people who don't think there should be a government. And traitors go against their own countries. But, no matter what name you give it, it is a horrible civil war. A civil war is fighting between people in the same country. Both sides spill the same red blood onto our soil. My heart breaks to think about it.

There have been crimes on both sides of this terrible fight. England has made us pay taxes without our agreeing to them. English soldiers have shot at us. The colonists have misbehaved, too. They poured English tea into Boston Harbor. They have tarred and feathered the tax collectors of the king and his government. Both sides are wrong.

There are many of us. We are Quakers, Shakers, Moravians, Mennonites, Amish, and others. We will not fight. We think protecting life is more important than problems with government.

Others believe war goes against what it means to be free. Many people came from England and other countries to the American colonies to escape wars. Some left because they were not allowed to practice their religions. These citizens just wish to be left alone, in safety and in peace.

We believe war is wicked and unhealthy. No matter what reasons we are given, we will stay neutral. Neutral means we will not take a side. We strongly urge you to be neutral, too. We will not send our sons away from home to take the lives of others! Peace, my friends, at all costs.

—Reverend Nathaniel Thomas

Words of a Neutralist: Let Us Live in Peace!

War is a very great evil. War causes death and destruction. In war, too many lives are lost. Our problems and differences must be worked out through peaceful discussion, compromise, and tolerance, or acceptance of differences. Problems cannot be solved through bloodshed.

In Philadelphia, Patriots tell us it is our job to fight against England for our independence. Meanwhile, the Loyalists tell us to fight for England, our mother country. The Loyalists say we must fight against the Patriots. They say the Patriots should not be rebelling against England.

The Patriots call this conflict, or fight, an American Revolution or a War of Independence. The Loyalists call it rebellion led by traitors and anarchists, or people who are against having a government. No matter what you name it, it is a horrible civil war. A civil war is fighting between people in the same country. It is neighbor killing neighbor, brother fighting brother. Both sides spill the same red blood.

There have been crimes on both sides of this terrible fight. England has taxed us without our agreement. English soldiers have shot at us. Many have died. On the other hand, colonists have been committing crimes, too. They poured English tea into Boston Harbor. They have tarred and feathered the tax collectors of the king and his government.

There are many of us who will not take up the sword. We are the Quakers, Shakers, Moravians, Mennonites, Amish, and others. Protecting life is more important to us than problems with governments.

There are others who refuse to make war. They believe it goes against the spirit of freedom. Many came from England and other countries to the American colonies to escape wars and religious persecution. These citizens want only to be left alone, in safety, and in peace.

We believe that all war is wicked and unhealthy. No matter what reasons we are given, we will remain neutral; we will not take a side. We strongly urge you to be neutral, too. We will not send our sons away to kill others or to leave their blood on battlefields! Peace, my friends, at all costs.

—Reverend Nathaniel Thomas

Name _____ Date _____

Use what you read in the passage to answer the questions.

1. Is the writer a Patriot, a Loyalist, or neither?

_____

_____

2. Where does the writer live?

_____

_____

3. How does the writer feel about war?

_____

_____

4. What is a civil war?

_____

_____

5. What is the difference between a Patriot and a Loyalist?

_____

_____

6. How does the writer think he can solve their differences?

_____

_____

7. What is an **anarchist**?

_____

_____

8. What does it mean to be **neutral**?

_____

_____

Lengthen the School Year Before It's Too Late!

Students in the United States are behind. Other countries are getting ahead. The U.S. kids need to spend more time in school. They are not getting the skills needed for today's jobs. Making the school year longer is one way to do this. Many students in the U.S. do nothing in the summer. Meanwhile, students in other countries work hard over the summer.

In the nineteenth century, summer was for farming. Kids had to work on the family farm in the summer. But times and needs have changed. Today there are very few family farms left. Some doctors study how children think and behave. They say children are happier when they have stuff to do. They are healthier. They are better behaved, too. Kids forget things they've learned in the summer. This is called "summer learning loss." Experts say students forget what they've learned. They forget at least one month of school over a summer.

Students in other countries have shorter vacations.

Japanese students	243 days per year in school
U.S. students	180 days per year in school

No wonder Japan is third in the world in science knowledge. In the twenty-first century, most jobs will need special training. The most needed **occupations** will be computer, math, technology, and health care jobs. To do these jobs, students must have strong math, science, and reading skills. U.S. students will have to meet tough standards.

There is a solution. U.S. students should be in school longer. Some schools already have made the school day longer. Other schools have added days to their school year. Studies show that the more time in school, the higher the test scores. Reports say reading test scores are higher when kids are in school all year.

Today, students in the United States have to compete for jobs. Students from around the world are taking jobs here. Let's help U.S. kids have a chance. Add more days to the school year. Keep students working on learning year-round. In the long run, they will be the ones who thank you most.

Lengthen the School Year Before It's Too Late!

Students in the United States need to spend more time in school. They are not getting the skills needed for today's jobs. Making the school year longer is one way to do this. Many students in the United States do nothing important during their summer vacations. Meanwhile, students in other countries are hard at work over the summer.

In the nineteenth century, schoolchildren had to work on the family farm in the summer. But times and needs have changed. Today there are very few family farms left in this country. Child psychologists study how children think and behave. They say children are happier and healthier when they have regular schedules. They are better behaved, too. Every week that students are not in school, they forget things they've learned. This is called "summer learning loss." Last year, a review of summer learning loss studies was published. The studies say students forget at least one month of instruction over a summer.

Students in other countries have shorter vacations. Japanese students are in school 243 days per year. In the United States students are in school for only 180 days per year. No wonder Japan is third in the world in science knowledge. In the twenty-first century, most occupations, or jobs, will be in the computer, mathematical, technical, and health care fields. To do these jobs, students must have strong math, science, and reading skills. If U.S. students want these jobs, they will have to meet tough standards.

There is a solution. U.S. students should be in school longer. Some schools already have made the school day longer. Other schools have added days to their school year. This makes their summer vacations shorter. Studies show that the more time in school, the higher the test scores. A report found that reading test scores improved when kids were in school all year.

Today, students in the United States have competition for jobs. Students from around the world are taking jobs here. U.S. children deserve a fighting chance to succeed. The twenty-first century is competitive. Add more days to the school year. Keep students focused on learning. In the long run, they will be the ones who thank you most.

Lengthen the School Year Before It's Too Late!

To have the skills needed for jobs today, students in the United States must spend more time in school. One way to do this is to make the school year longer. Many students in the United States waste their summer vacations. Meanwhile, students in other countries are hard at work during the summer. In the nineteenth century, schoolchildren had to work the family farm come summertime. But times and needs have changed. Today there are very few family farms in this country.

Child psychologists, or doctors, argue that children are happier, healthier, and better behaved when they have regular schedules, as in school. They explain that every week students are not in school, they forget some of what they learned. This is known as "summer learning loss." Last year, an analysis, or review, of summer learning loss studies was published. The studies found that summer learning loss equals at least one month of instruction. Students in other countries don't seem to suffer from shorter vacations. Japanese students attend school 243 days per year. In comparison, U.S. students are in school for only 180 days per year. It's no wonder that Japan ranked third in scientific literacy.

The situation will have a serious effect on the future. In the twenty-first century, most occupations, or jobs, will be in the computer, mathematical, technical, and health care fields. To do these jobs, students must have strong math, science, and literacy skills. If U.S. students want these jobs, they will have to meet tough standards.

There is a solution. Students should be in school longer. Some schools already have made the school day longer. Other schools have added days to their school calendar and made their summer vacations much shorter. Studies show that more time spent in the classroom correlates, or connects directly with, higher achievement scores. A report found that reading test scores went up 19.3 percent when grade school students were in school all year.

Today, students are not just competing with other U.S. students for employment opportunities, or jobs. They are competing with students from around the world. And students from other countries are winning. Parents and teachers owe their children a chance to succeed in the competitive twenty-first-century economy. Add more days to the school year. In the long run, they will be the ones who thank you most.

●●●

Name _____ Date _____

Use what you read in the passage to answer the questions.

1. What does the word **occupation** mean?

_____

_____

2. What is the writer's position?

_____

_____

3. Why didn't children go to school in the summer in the nineteenth century?

_____

_____

4. Who argues that children need structure?

_____

_____

5. Summer learning loss is equal to how much instruction time each year?

_____

_____

6. Why does the writer mention other studies and reports in the letter?

_____

_____

7. What are two job fields that are growing in the twenty-first century?

_____

_____

8. Who attends school for more days: students in the United States or Japan?

_____

_____

Unit 8 Mini-Lesson
Book and Film Reviews

What is a review?

A review is a summary of comments and opinions about a book or film. Writers of reviews tell what happens in the story and share their opinion about it. They tell what is good about the story and what might be bad or weak. They use details from the story to support their opinions.

What is the purpose of a review?

People write reviews to share with others the joys of stories. Many people like to know about a book before they read it or a film before they see it. That way they know if it is a right match for them. Does the subject interest them? A review helps the reader decide whether to read a book or see a film.

Who is the audience for a review?

The audience for the review depends on the audience for the book or film, as well as the audience where the review will be printed. The audience will be people interested in that subject. The reviewer writes to all the people who might be interested in the book or film.

How do you read a review?

Pay attention to the plot, characters, and subject matter. Does the story line appeal to you? Did it interest the reviewer? How can you tell? What did the reviewer like? What did the reviewer dislike? Did the writer give good reasons for these opinions? Do you want to read the book or watch the film now?

Describes the main setting, main characters, and basic plot of the story

Gives the title and information about the author or director

Does NOT give away any surprises or the ending

Film or Book Review

Includes short quotes from the book or film to illustrate a point

Gives opinions on the strengths and weaknesses of the book or film

Leaves questions in the reader's mind so they will want to read the book or see the film

Stuart Little

E. B. White is an author. One night he had a dream. The dream was about a little boy. The little boy looked like a mouse. White decided to write a few adventures about this mouse. He put the stories in a drawer. Twenty years later, he wrote more stories. Then he put the stories together in a book. The book was *Stuart Little*. It was published in 1945.

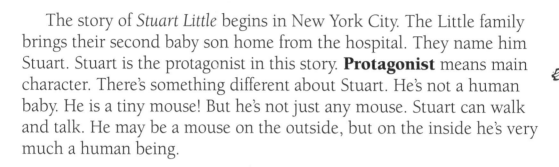

NIX ON SWIPING ANYTHING ABSOLUTELY NO BEING MEAN!

The story of *Stuart Little* begins in New York City. The Little family brings their second baby son home from the hospital. They name him Stuart. Stuart is the protagonist in this story. **Protagonist** means main character. There's something different about Stuart. He's not a human baby. He is a tiny mouse! But he's not just any mouse. Stuart can walk and talk. He may be a mouse on the outside, but on the inside he's very much a human being.

Stuart Little is the story of someone on a search. Nothing stops Stuart even though he is different from everyone else. He is determined to prove himself time after time. In the end, Stuart shows what it means to be a friend. Some parts of *Stuart Little* are funny. In one of my favorite parts, Stuart becomes friends with Dr. Carey. Dr. Carey is a dentist. He owns a miniature, or very tiny, boat called *Wasp*. He races *Wasp* against other boats at a pond in Central Park. Look for the conversation between Dr. Carey and Stuart.

Stuart is a magnificent character. Magnificent means wonderful. He's also sympathetic. That means kind and understanding. He's much smarter than his brother or even his parents. Stuart is not perfect. I like that about him. Stuart finally meets a girl his size, Miss Harriet Ames. Stuart invites her on a canoe ride. But when the canoe falls apart, Stuart falls apart, too. He moans and groans. No wonder the girl walks away!

One problem with the book has to do with the plot. The plot is the main story. There are too many things we never find out. Stuart runs away from home to find his best friend, the bird Margalo. He is also looking for his fortune. Some people along the way give him hints on where to go. But we never find out what happens. All we find out is that Stuart is heading north. That is not a good ending to me.

Still, Stuart is a magical character. I think everyone should meet him.

Stuart Little

One night author E. B. White had a dream. The dream was about a little boy who looked like a mouse. The dream seemed vivid, or real. So White decided to write a few adventures about this mouse. He put the stories in a drawer. Twenty years later, he wrote more stories. Then he collected all the stories into a book, *Stuart Little*. It was published in 1945.

The story of *Stuart Little* begins in New York City. The wonderful Little family brings their second baby son home from the hospital. They name him Stuart. But there's something different about Stuart. He's not a human baby. Instead, he is a tiny mouse. Yet he's not like any mouse you or I have ever seen. This little mouse can walk and talk. White's protagonist, or main character, may be a mouse on the outside, but on the inside he's very human.

Stuart Little is the story of someone on a quest, or search. Nothing stops Stuart even though he is different from everyone else. He is always determined to prove himself. And in the end, he shows what it means to be a friend. Some parts of *Stuart Little* are very funny. In one of my favorite parts, Stuart becomes friends with Dr. Paul Carey. Dr. Paul Carey is a dentist. He owns a miniature boat called *Wasp*. He races against other boats in a Central Park pond. Look for the conversation between Dr. Carey and Stuart.

Stuart is a magnificent, or wonderful, character. He's also sympathetic. That means kind and understanding. He's much smarter than his brother or even his parents. I liked that he wasn't perfect. When Stuart finally gets a chance to meet a girl his size (Miss Harriet Ames), he invites her on a canoe ride. When the canoe falls apart, so does Stuart. He moans and groans. No wonder the girl walks away. But who can't recognize that feeling?

The book has one problem. The plot, or main part of story, has loose ends. Stuart runs away from home to find his best friend, the bird Margalo. He is also seeking his fortune. Some people along the way give him hints on where to go. But we never discover what happens. Does he find Margalo? Does he find his fortune? All we know in the end is that Stuart is heading north. That is not a satisfying ending. Still, Stuart is a magical character. I think everyone should meet him.

Stuart Little

One night author E. B. White had a dream. The dream was about a little boy who looked like a mouse. The dream was so vivid that White decided to write a few adventures about this mouse. He put the stories in a drawer and saved them for his nieces and nephews. Twenty years later, he expanded and collected all the stories into the book *Stuart Little*, published in 1945.

The book begins in New York City. The wonderful Little family brings their second baby son, whom they've named Stuart, home from the hospital. But there's something different about Stuart. He's not a human baby. Instead, he is a tiny mouse. Yet he's not like any mouse you or I have ever seen. This little mouse can walk upright and talk. White's protagonist may be a mouse on the outside, but on the inside he's ultrahuman.

Stuart Little is the story of someone on a quest. Though he is different from everyone else, Stuart lets nothing stop him. He is always determined to prove himself. And in the end, he shows what being a friend is all about. Some parts of *Stuart Little* are very funny. In one of my favorite parts, Stuart befriends Dr. Paul Carey. This dentist owns a miniature boat called *Wasp* that he races against other boats in a Central Park pond. Look for the conversation between Dr. Carey and Stuart.

Stuart himself is a magnificent and sympathetic character. He's much smarter than his brother or even his parents. And he's thoughtful, kind, and independent. And I liked that he wasn't perfect, too. When he finally gets a chance to meet a girl his size (Miss Harriet Ames), he invites her on a canoe ride and gets ready for the big date. When the canoe falls apart, so does Stuart. He moans and groans. No wonder the girl walks away from Stuart. But who can't identify with that?

One problem with the book is that the plot has loose ends. Stuart runs away from home for good to find his best friend, the bird Margalo, and also to seek his fortune. Some people along the way give him hints on where to go. But we never discover what happens. Does he find Margalo? Does he find his fortune? All we know in the end is that Stuart is heading north, and that is not a satisfying ending to me. Still, Stuart is a magical character, and I think everyone should meet him.

Name _____ Date _____

Use what you read in the passage to answer the questions.

1. What book is reviewed?

_____

_____

2. Who is the author of the book?

_____

_____

3. Who is the **protagonist**, or main character, in the book?

_____

_____

4. In what way is Stuart Little like a human being?

_____

_____

5. What does the author like about the main character?

_____

_____

6. What doesn't the writer like about the book?

_____

_____

7. What is the writer's purpose in writing this review?

_____

_____

8. Why would or wouldn't you read this book?

_____

_____

Charlotte's Web

There are many miracles in this funny and charming movie. The movie is based on the book *Charlotte's Web* by E. B. White.

This movie was made in 2006. It is also called *Charlotte's Web*. A cute little pig named Wilbur is going to be killed. But a smart spider named Charlotte and her barnyard friends help Wilbur. Charlotte's idea is to weave words like "terrific" into her spiderweb. The words describe Wilbur. The pig becomes famous all over the county.

Director Gary Winick makes the movie exciting. First, he uses live action. Live action means that you use real actors. Second, he has big stars playing the parts. Computer animation is used for the scenes with animals. The animation makes the animals seem as if they can talk. There is one problem. Charlotte does not look like a real spider. She is made softer so she is less scary. I think this was a mistake. Children can see beyond what Charlotte looks like on the outside. They are able to understand that she is beautiful on the inside.

The actress Dakota Fanning is great in the part of Fern. In the book, Fern doesn't stand up for herself enough. But Fanning plays the little girl as smart and spunky. She does a great job talking her father into keeping the little pig. The dad knows he's helpless against Fern. He gives up without much of a fight. It was a great idea for Winick to use famous actors for the voices of the animals. They were all terrific. Julia Roberts is the voice of Charlotte. Her kind voice is perfect for the part.

Be warned. The movie has lots of funny moments that the book does not. Purists, or people who like things exactly as they were meant, will be annoyed. But I liked the movie's comic relief. In the barn, the animals drool, burp, and make other silly noises. The book is more serious.

The movie is serious, too. It explores friendship. Charlotte is a best friend. She has her own problems, but she never leaves Wilbur. This is especially true when he needs her most. And Wilbur returns the favor. He becomes Charlotte's best friend in the end.

Winick gets this movie right. It has just the correct mixture of funny, sweet, and sad to make it enjoyable. Gather up the family. Get some candy and popcorn and enjoy *Charlotte's Web*.

Charlotte's Web

There are many miracles in this funny and charming re-creation of the book *Charlotte's Web* by E. B. White. This movie, also called *Charlotte's Web*, was made in 2006. A cute pig named Wilbur is saved from a terrible fate. A clever spider, Charlotte, and her barnyard friends help Wilbur. Charlotte's strategy, or idea, is to weave words like "terrific" into her spiderweb to describe Wilbur. The pig becomes famous all over the county.

Director Gary Winick uses live action, not cartoons, and big stars to make the movie exciting. The animal shots are enhanced, or made better, with computer animation. The animation makes the barnyard creatures seem as if they can talk. There is one problem. Charlotte does not look like a real spider. The filmmakers softened her to make Charlotte less scary. I think this was a mistake. They should have trusted young viewers to see beyond what Charlotte looks like on the outside. Children are able to understand that she is beautiful on the inside.

The actress Dakota Fanning does a great job as Fern. In the book, Fern doesn't assert herself, or stand up for herself, enough. But Fanning plays the little girl as smart and spunky. She does a great job talking her father into keeping the little pig. The dad knows he's helpless against her. Winick was smart to hire famous actors to be the voices of the animals. They were all terrific. Julia Roberts is the voice of Charlotte. Her kind, benevolent voice is perfect for the part.

Be warned. The movie has lots of comic, or funny, moments that the book does not. Purists, or people who like things exactly as they were meant, will be annoyed. But I liked the movie's comic relief. There's plenty of funny conversations and some silly humor. In the barn, the animals drool, burp, and make other silly noises.

But the movie is also serious. It explores different levels of friendship. Charlotte is a best friend. Although she has her own problems, she never leaves Wilbur, especially when he needs her most. And Wilbur returns the favor. He becomes Charlotte's best friend.

Winick gets this movie right. It has just the correct mixture of funny, sweet, and sad to make it enjoyable. So gather up the family. Get some candy and popcorn and enjoy *Charlotte's Web*.

Charlotte's Web

There are many miracles in store in this funny and charming re-creation of the E. B. White book *Charlotte's Web*. This movie, with the same title, was produced in 2006. A cute little pig named Wilbur is saved from a terrible fate by the clever spider Charlotte and her barnyard friends. Charlotte's strategy is to weave words like "radiant" and "terrific" into her spiderweb to describe Wilbur. The pig becomes a celebrity for the entire county.

Director Gary Winick brings the excitement of live action and a star-filled cast to his movie. The animal shots are enhanced with computer animation. That makes all the barnyard creatures seem as if they can really talk. There is one problem. Charlotte does not look like a real spider. The filmmakers softened her looks to make her appear less scary to children, which I think was a mistake. They should have trusted young viewers to see beyond Charlotte's natural exterior—to appreciate her inner beauty.

Winick gets a great performance out of Dakota Fanning as Fern. In the book, Fern doesn't assert herself enough, but Fanning plays the little girl as smart and spunky. Watch how she talks her father into keeping the little pig. The dad knows he's helpless against her. Winick smartly hired famous actors to be the voices of the animals, and they were terrific. Julia Roberts is a perfect Charlotte, with a kind, benevolent voice.

Be warned. Lots of comic touches have been added to this story. Purists who like White's book and don't want any changes will be annoyed. But I appreciated the movie's occasional comic relief. There's plenty of funny dialogue and some silly humor. In the barn, the animals drool, burp, and make other silly noises that are not in the spirit of the book.

But the movie also makes serious points. It explores different levels of friendship. Charlotte is a best friend. Although she has her own problems, she never abandons Wilbur. And Wilbur returns the favor. He becomes her best friend.

Winick gets this movie right. It has just the correct mixture of funny, sweet, and sad to make it enjoyable to watch. So gather up the family. Get some sweet candy and salty popcorn and enjoy *Charlotte's Web*.

Name _____ Date _____

Use what you read in the passage to answer the questions.

1. What is the name of the movie? Who wrote the book?

_____

_____

2. Who is Wilbur?

_____

_____

3. How is the part of Fern different in the book than in the movie?

_____

_____

4. What is the one problem the reviewer has with the movie?

_____

_____

5. Why might purists not like the movie?

_____

_____

6. Who is Wilbur's best friend?

_____

_____

7. What does the reviewer think of Julia Roberts's performance?

_____

_____

8. Would this review make you want to see the movie? Why or why not?

_____

_____

Unit 9 Mini-Lesson
Advertisements

What is an advertisement?

An advertisement, or "ad," is a form of opinion/argument text. It may include writing, images, or both. The ad writer tries to persuade the audience to buy or do something.

What is the purpose of an advertisement?

People write advertisements to sell products. The goal of an ad is to persuade others to buy, do, or use certain goods or services. Some ads explain how a product works or tell why one product is better than another. Other ads explain how a product or service can solve a problem or make people's lives better. Often, ads try to entertain people or make a lasting impression in some way so that people will remember to buy the product.

Who is the audience for an advertisement?

The audience for an advertisement is the consumer, or person who buys things. The type of consumer audience depends on the product or service being sold. It also depends on where the ad is printed. The audience will be people interested in that product.

How do you read an advertisement?

Ask yourself: *What is the product or service being sold? How is the writer trying to sell it? Does the ad writer do a good job? Does the ad leave a lasting impression? Does the writer convince you that you want or perhaps even need the product?*

Describes why a product or service is worth buying/using

Targets a specific consumer audience based on where the ad is presented

Gives the name and information about a product and where to buy it

Gives opinions on the strengths of a product or service

Advertisement

May include any of the following text structures: description, main idea and supporting facts and details, compare and contrast, problem/solution, cause and effect

May include endorsements, awards, or notable mentions that the product has won

Leaves a lasting impression so consumers will want to buy the product

BLAST Toothpaste

Hey, kids! Do you hate to brush your teeth?

Do you want to be left alone? Tired of hearing "Did you brush your teeth?"

If so, then you need BLAST. BLAST is toothpaste. BLAST is BEST. Do you want to know why? Well, you only have to use it once a week! BLAST on Sunday. No need to brush until next Sunday. No kidding! BLAST has a secret formula. It has mouth-friendly acids. The acids eat away tartar and plaque. Your teeth stay clean for seven days.

So don't just brush your teeth. You need to BLAST your teeth. Try BLAST once a week. You will be happy you did.

Save $1 with this ad!

BLAST Toothpaste

Hey, kids! Do you hate to brush your teeth?

Do you want to be left alone? Are you tired of hearing "Did you brush your teeth?" from your nagging parents?

If so, then you need BLAST toothpaste. BLAST is BEST because you only have to use BLAST once a week! BLAST on Sunday and then there is no need to brush until next Sunday. BLAST has a secret formula of mouth-friendly acids. The acids strip away tartar and plaque. Your teeth stay clean for seven days, no kidding!

So don't just brush your teeth; BLAST your teeth. Try BLAST once a week, and you will be happy you did.

Save $1 off your first purchase with this ad!

BLAST Toothpaste

Hey, kids! Do you hate to brush your teeth?

Don't you wish you could fall into bed at night without hearing "Did you brush your teeth?" from your parents?

If so, then you need BLAST toothpaste. BLAST is BEST because you only have to use it once a week! BLAST on Sunday and you won't need to brush your teeth again until the next Sunday. BLAST has a secret formula of mouth-friendly acids that strip away all tartar and plaque. Your teeth stay spotless for seven days.

So don't just brush your teeth—BLAST your teeth. Try once-a-week BLAST toothpaste.

Get $1 off your first tube of BLAST with this ad!

Name _____ Date _____

Use what you read in the passage to answer the questions.

1. How many days does BLAST keep teeth clean?

_____

_____

2. List at least one way BLAST is better than regular toothpastes.

_____

_____

3. Why do you think the product name is written in all capital letters?

_____

_____

4. What does the word "blast" normally mean?

_____

_____

5. What are the ingredients in BLAST?

_____

_____

6. What is the main purpose of this ad?

_____

_____

7. What is the purpose of all the questions at the beginning of the ad?

_____

_____

8. Would you buy BLAST? Why or why not?

_____

_____

Vita-Shake

Vita-Shake is healthy! It is tasty. And everyone wants it!

Do you feel tired? Do you wish you could sleep late each day?

Do you feel tired in the afternoon?

Do you need coffees, colas, or energy drinks? Do they help you wake up in the afternoon?

Do you want to feel good and strong again?

Did you say yes to any of these questions? Then you need Vita-Shake. Vita-Shake is a creamy shake. It does not have milk. But it has all the vitamins and minerals you need. It will give you health. It will make you happy. Just defrost the container for thirty minutes on the counter. Or if you are in a hurry, microwave it for sixty seconds. Pop the top and you have a yummy, smooth treat. There's no reason to feel guilty. It is good for your body. We promise you will get better skin, hair, and nails. And you will feel well. Just try Vita-Shake for one month. You will notice a difference.

Vita-Shake. Shake up your energy!

Vita-Shake

Vita-Shake—It is the healthy sensation that's sweeping the nation!

Do you feel tired?

Is it hard to get out of bed in the morning?

Do you feel a midday slump in the afternoon?

Are you depending on coffees, colas, and/or energy drinks to get you through the day?

Do you want to feel good and strong again?

If you said yes to any of these questions, then you need Vita-Shake. Vita-Shake is a creamy, nondairy shake that has all the vitamins and minerals you need for health and happiness. Just defrost the patented container for thirty minutes on the counter. Or if you are in a hurry, microwave the container for sixty seconds. Pop the top and you have a luscious, smooth treat that is guilt-free and good for your body. You are guaranteed to see improvements in your skin, hair, nails, and well-being after just one month on Vita-Shake.

Vita-Shake. Shake up your energy!

Vita-Shake

Vita-Shake—It is the healthy sensation that's sweeping the nation!

Do you feel exhausted?

Is it impossible to drag yourself out of bed in the morning?

Do you feel a midday slump in the afternoon that has you yawning and distracted?

Are you depending on coffees, colas, and/or energy drinks to help you survive the day?

Do you want to feel healthy and motivated again?

If you said yes to any of these questions, then you need Vita-Shake. Vita-Shake is a creamy, nondairy shake that has all of the vitamins and minerals necessary for radiant health. Just defrost the patented faux-glass container for thirty minutes on the counter. Or if you are in a hurry, microwave the container for sixty seconds. Pop the top and you have a luscious, smooth treat that is guilt-free and nutritious. You are guaranteed to see improvements in your skin, hair, nails, and overall well-being after just one month on the Vita-Shake plan.

Vita-Shake. Shake up your energy!

●●●

Name _____ Date _____

Use what you read in the passage to answer the questions.

1. What is Vita-Shake?

_____

_____

2. What does Vita-Shake help you do?

_____

_____

3. How is Vita-Shake different from other energy drinks?

_____

_____

4. What is in Vita-Shake?

_____

_____

5. How is Vita-Shake kept—in the refrigerator, freezer, or cabinet?

_____

_____

6. What is Vita-Shake guaranteed to do?

_____

_____

7. What purpose do all the questions serve at the beginning of the ad?

_____

_____

8. Would you buy Vita-Shake? Why or why not?

_____

_____

Unit 10 Mini-Lesson
Speeches

What is a speech?

A speech is a written document that is recited or read aloud. A speech tries to convince readers to believe or do something. A speech, like other opinion/argument texts, often has a strong point of view about an idea or a problem. It includes facts and examples to support an opinion, and it usually suggests a solution.

What is the purpose of a speech?

People write speeches to "sway," or change the minds of, their audience. They want their audience to see their points of view. They may want to motivate, or encourage people to take action, too. The purpose of a political speech might be to change public opinion or persuade people to vote for something or someone. Other speeches are written to inspire, celebrate, or simply thank people.

Who is the audience for a speech?

People write speeches for all types of occasions, including political rallies, award ceremonies, weddings, funerals, and even birthday parties. People write speeches to share their views and tell others about something they believe in. They may write a speech to gain support for a person or a cause. They may also write a speech to convince their audience to act in favor or against something.

How do you read (or listen to) a speech?

Keep in mind that the speaker or speechwriter wants you to support a particular position. Ask yourself: *What is this person's position, or opinion? Does she support it with facts and good reasons? Do I agree with the speaker?* Good speechwriters know their audience. They use facts and reasons that might sway the audience in their favor. They also read the speech aloud several times to make sure that the words are powerful and flow when spoken.

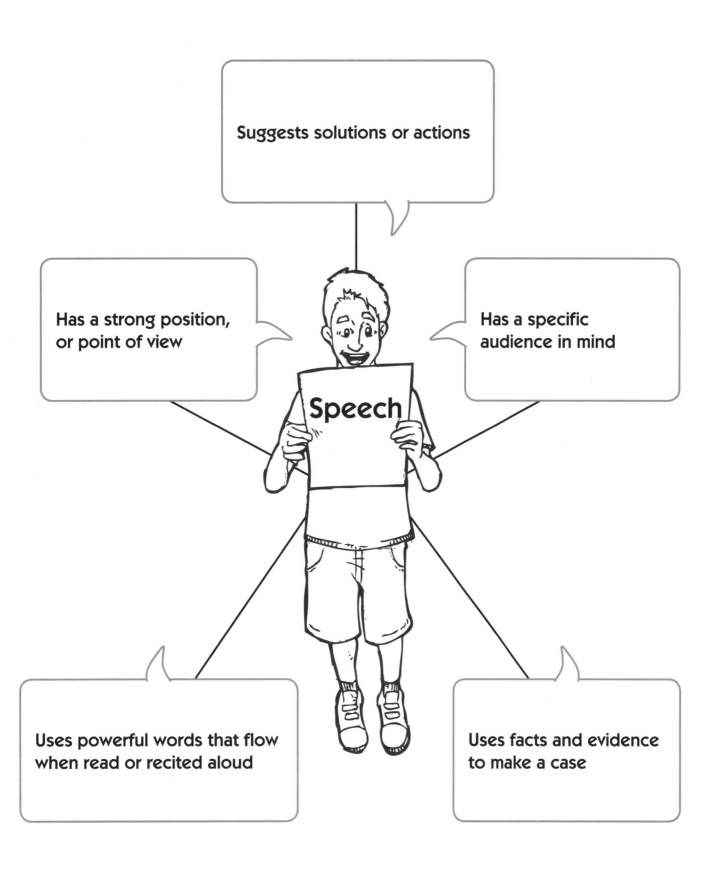

My Fellow Citizens,

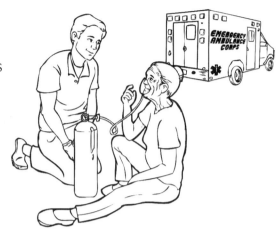

Welcome to the Community Forum. Tonight's discussion is about the problem of emergency health care in our town. There is none. I think we should sell the old fairgrounds. We should build an emergency health-care center. I need to discuss this topic. It's not just because I'm your elected chairman. But I also have an important story to tell.

On Sunday I was taking a walk. My wife, Mimi, was with me. She began to feel dizzy. She could not breathe well. Mimi is eighty-two years old. I am eighty-three. I was very worried. Our doctor's office is closed on the weekends. And the volunteer ambulance does not come to our county. So I drove my wife to a hospital. The ride took more than an hour. There was lots of traffic. We had to wait forty-five minutes to see a doctor. The good news is that Mimi is okay. The bad news could be next time. If Mimi had gotten worse, she might have been in real trouble. We may not have had help in time.

Some people have to travel too far for health care. Too many deaths happen each year. This can be prevented. We need trained emergency people in our community. We need ambulances. Many people agree with me. Senior citizens agree. Parents of young children agree. Councilmember Adams says we can train volunteers in a few years. But a few years is too long. We need emergency ambulances now! We need an emergency room now! We need trained doctors and nurses now!

Mr. Adams wants to build a mall on the old fairgrounds. I support selling the old fairgrounds. I'm okay with building a new mall. But we need an emergency room, too. Our town does need stores, restaurants, and movie theaters. It needs the jobs that come with these places. But life is more important. You can't enjoy stores if you are dead!

I hope you'll sign the petition. I am sending it around the crowd now. Together we can build a better and safer community. We can start by demanding the much-needed services. We deserve them.

Thank you for listening. Have a good evening.

My Fellow Citizens,

Welcome to the Community Forum. Tonight's discussion is about the problem of emergency health care in our town. There is none. I think we should sell the old fairgrounds and build an emergency health-care center. I want to discuss this topic not just as your elected chairman, but because I have an important story to tell.

Last Sunday, my wife and I were taking our evening walk. Her name is Mimi. She began to feel dizzy. She was short of breath, too. Mimi is eighty-two and I am eighty-three. I was very concerned. Our doctor's office is closed on the weekends. And the volunteer ambulance does not come to our county. So I drove my wife to the hospital. The ride took more than an hour because of the weekend traffic. Then we had to wait another forty-five minutes to see a doctor. The good news is that Mimi's condition was not serious. She has fully recovered. She'll be fine. The bad news is that if Mimi had been seriously ill, she might not have gotten the treatment she needed in time.

Too many deaths happen each year because of how far people must travel to get the medical care they need. We need a trained emergency ambulance corps in our community. Many senior citizens and parents of young children are as concerned as I am. Councilmember Adams says that we can begin a program to train volunteers in a few years. But a few years is too long. We need emergency ambulances now! We need an emergency clinic now! We need trained medical professionals, such as doctors and nurses, now!

Mr. Adams wants to build a mall on the old fairgrounds. I support selling the old fairgrounds to build a new mall. But I agree with the plan only if an emergency clinic and a trained emergency ambulance corps are part of the plan. There also needs to be a garage for an ambulance. Our town does need stores, restaurants, movie theaters, and the jobs that come with them. But these aren't important if you're not alive to enjoy them.

I hope you'll sign the petition that I am sending around the crowd now. Together we can build a better and safer community. We can start by demanding the much-needed services that we deserve.

Thank you for listening, and have a good evening.

My Fellow Citizens,

Welcome to the Community Forum. For tonight's discussion I want to talk to you about getting better emergency health care for our town. I think we should use the old fairgrounds to build an emergency health-care center. I want to discuss this topic not just as your elected chair, but because I have an important story to tell.

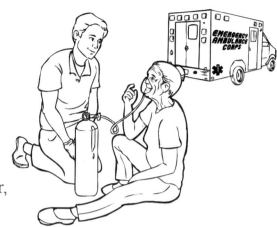

Last Sunday, my wife Mimi and I were taking our evening walk. Mimi began to feel dizzy and she was short of breath. She is eighty-two and I am eighty-three. As you can imagine, I was very concerned. Our doctor's office is closed on the weekends and the volunteer ambulance does not come to our county. So I drove my wife to the hospital. The ride took more than an hour because of the weekend traffic. Then we were forced to wait another forty-five minutes to see a doctor. The good news is that Mimi's condition was not serious. She has fully recovered and will be fine. The bad news is that if she had been seriously ill, she might not have gotten the treatment she needed in time.

Too many deaths happen each year because of the distance people have to travel to get the medical care they need. We need a trained emergency ambulance corps to serve our community. Many senior citizens and parents of young children share my concern. Councilmember Adams says that we can begin a program to train volunteers in a few years. But a few years is too long. We need emergency ambulances now! We need an emergency clinic with trained medical professionals, such as doctors and nurses, now!

Mr. Adams wants to build a mall on the old fairgrounds. I support selling the old fairgrounds to build a new mall. But I agree with the plan only if an emergency clinic and a trained emergency ambulance corps are part of the plan. There also needs to be a garage for an ambulance. Our town does need stores, restaurants, movie theaters, and the jobs that come with them. But these aren't important if you're not alive to enjoy them.

I hope you'll support the petition that I am sending around the crowd now. Together we can build a better and safer community. We can start by demanding the much-needed services that we deserve.

Thank you for listening. Have a good evening.

Name _____ Date _____

Use what you read in the passage to answer the questions.

1. Who is giving this speech?

_____

_____

2. Who is listening to the speech?

_____

_____

3. What does the person giving the speech want?

_____

_____

4. Who is Mimi? What happened to her?

_____

_____

5. Why did it take so long to get Mimi to the hospital?

_____

_____

6. Why do you think the speech giver supports the mall?

_____

_____

7. Where does the speech giver suggest the emergency room/clinic be built?

_____

_____

8. Are you convinced by the speech? Why or why not?

_____

_____

Welcome, Valley Farmers!

Thank you for coming this afternoon. Farmer Laura is this year's Farmer of the Year. She has the most successful organic farm in the valley. I want to thank Farmer Laura. Climate change is a big problem. Farmer Laura is doing something to solve it. Farmer Laura is a great model for all of us. We should all watch and learn from Farmer Laura.

We need to be careful in the next 100 years. The temperature of our planet cannot rise even a little. Any temperature change is bad for Earth. Some parts of the world will have too little rain. Drought occurs when the weather is very dry. Other parts of the world will have too much rain. There could be terrible winds and flooding. The temperature change may make it hard to grow crops. If there are no crops, people will go hungry.

People waste energy. We know how large farms make this problem worse. We use oil in farm equipment. We use oil for trucks to ship food. The oil makes greenhouse gases. The gas from the oil is bad. It traps the sun's heat in our atmosphere. This causes our planet to warm up.

Organic farming burns less fossil fuel. That means less harmful carbon dioxide gas is in the air. A study found that organic farming keeps more carbon in the soil. That is good.

All farmers should do like Farmer Laura. All farmers should have an eco-friendly organic farm. Like Farmer Laura, we need to think globally and act locally. We need to take care of our world. We need to take care of our community. I encourage every farmer to visit Laura's farm. It will give you ideas. Her ideas will help you save money and the planet! Together, let's help solve the problem of global climate change.

LAURA'S ORGANIC FARM
Winner of Farmer
of the Year Award

Welcome, Valley Farmers!

Thank you for coming this afternoon. Farmer Laura is this year's Farmer of the Year. She is Farmer of the Year for having the most successful organic farm in the valley. I want to thank Farmer Laura for what she's doing. Global climate change is a serious problem. Farmer Laura is doing something to solve it. Farmer Laura is a great model for all of us. We should all start using practices like the ones Farmer Laura uses on her farm.

In the next 100 years, if the temperature of our planet rises even just a little, it will be very bad for Earth. Some parts of the world will have drought. Drought occurs when the weather is very dry. Other parts of the world could have terrible winds, rain, and flooding. Climate change could make it hard for farmers to grow crops. If there are no crops, people all over the world could starve.

People waste too much energy. We know how large farms make this problem worse. We use oil for running farm equipment and shipping food. The oil makes greenhouse gases. The gases trap the sun's heat in our atmosphere. This causes our planet to warm up.

Organic farming burns less fossil fuel. That means less harmful carbon dioxide gas is in the air. A study by an institute finds that organic farming keeps more carbon in the soil. All farmers should be following what Farmer Laura does on her organic farm. Like Farmer Laura, we need to think globally and act locally. I encourage every farmer to visit Laura's farm. Go see some of her eco-friendly methods in action. It may give you ideas on how you can save money and the planet! Together, let's help solve the problem of global climate change.

LAURA'S ORGANIC FARM
Winner of Farmer
of the Year Award

Welcome, Valley Farmers!

Thank you for joining us this afternoon. We are here to honor Farmer Laura as Farmer of the Year. She has earned this year's title by creating the most successful organic farm in the valley. I want to personally thank Farmer Laura. Global climate change is a serious problem. Farmer Laura is doing something to solve it. Everyone should follow in Farmer Laura's low-carbon footprints. By that I mean we should all start farming like Farmer Laura.

If the temperature of our planet rises just several degrees in the next 100 years, it will be very bad for Earth. Some parts of the world will have drought, or very dry weather. Other parts of the world could have terrible winds, rain, and flooding. Climates could change so that farmers would not be able to grow their crops. If that happens, people all over the world could face starvation.

People waste too much energy. As farmers we know how large farms make this problem worse. Running farm equipment and shipping food use oil. The oil produces greenhouse gases that trap the sun's heat in our atmosphere. This causes our planet to warm up.

Organic farming burns less fossil fuel. That means less harmful carbon dioxide gas in the air. And according to a study by the Rodale Institute, organic farming keeps more carbon in the soil. All farmers should be doing what Farmer Laura is doing with her eco-friendly organic farm. Let's start to think globally and act locally. I encourage every farmer to visit Laura's farm. Go see some of her eco-friendly methods in action. It may give you ideas on how you too can save money and the planet! Together, let's help solve the problem of global climate change.

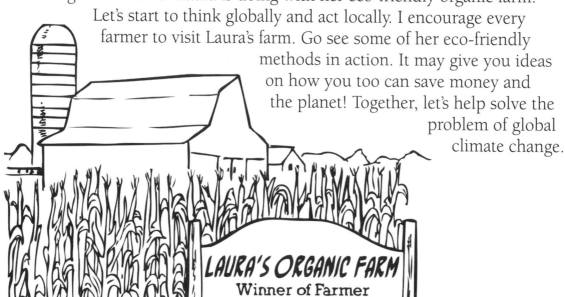

LAURA'S ORGANIC FARM
Winner of Farmer
of the Year Award

Name _____ Date _____

Use what you read in the passage to answer the questions.

1. Who is listening to the speech?

_____

_____

2. Who is being honored and why?

_____

_____

3. Why does the speaker encourage the farmers to visit Farmer Laura's farm?

_____

_____

4. What are some effects of rising temperatures?

_____

_____

5. What do farmers use oil for?

_____

_____

6. What could happen if farmers can't grow their crops?

_____

_____

7. Organic farming burns less . . .

_____

_____

8. Farmer Laura deserves the title Farmer of the Year because . . .

_____

_____

Answer Key

Unit 1 Personal Narrative I
page 13

1. Exciting to join their father in New York and scary for the voyage across the sea
2. New York
3. Because they do not have enough money
4. The writer is scared of the boat sinking and doesn't know how to swim very well.
5. The writer's parents have been in America since the writer was two.
6. Answers may vary. (Example: amazed)
7. The apartment has a kitchen, a bedroom, a living room, electric lights, and its own bathroom.
8. The writer was too young when his father left to remember him.

Unit 1 Personal Narrative II
page 17

1. Because Great Britain was preparing for war with Germany
2. Across the Atlantic Ocean
3. 1,102 passengers
4. Because of the German submarines nearby
5. A torpedo hit the ship.
6. She doesn't take a life jacket and blanket so that other people can have them.
7. More than seven hours; The sea is choppy.
8. Afraid. She calls the ladder "long" and "scary."

Unit 2 Realistic Fiction I
page 23

1. On a screened-in porch on a drizzly summer day
2. Maria, Jake, Cai, and Linda
3. Maria
4. Tossing, turning, snorting, snoring
5. Strong and speedy
6. His shoulders were slumping lower and lower; He pet his dog Tucker.
7. He yells at Linda.
8. Cai teaches Jake to play Scrabble®.

Unit 2 Realistic Fiction II
page 27

1. The dog Buff
2. Hiding in fear
3. Because he didn't want Buff to be taken away
4. Because it doesn't work
5. Because they offer to help buy Buff a toy
6. On sale
7. Answers may vary. (Example: "like little clouds on the carpet")
8. Buff keeps chewing on items in the house. The solution is to give him a toy to chew on.

Answer Key

Unit 3 Historical Fiction I
page 33

1. Engineer
2. They traveled to the United States together and sold fireworks together.
3. Utah
4. The dangerous conditions on the side of the mountain
5. Combination of chemicals
6. To cut through the mountain faster
7. Because an earlier explosion nearly killed three men
8. He wraps the nitroglycerin in a paper tube and adds a longer fuse.

Unit 3 Historical Fiction II
page 37

1. A guard at the Alamo
2. The Alamo in San Antonio, Texas
3. The Mexican Army
4. A church
5. Continued
6. He is sick.
7. He makes sure to keep the women and children safe.
8. So he won't endanger the others

Unit 4 Science Fiction I
page 43

1. A virtual 21st-century kid
2. 2512
3. A 3-D picture
4. Kansas has oceans.
5. Massive use of fossil fuels and the using up of Earth's resources
6. The oceans rose over farmland and cities.
7. Smokey Mountains
8. Using wind, solar, and hydropower efficiently

Unit 4 Science Fiction II
page 47

1. App of the Year
2. An Everything Tech or E.T.
3. The Information Cloud
4. Media/reporters
5. To provide background
6. Encourages people to do the right things
7. Grab one's attention
8. The Encouragement Patch kept bothering everyone.

Answer Key

Unit 5 Early Explorers
page 55

1. Gold
2. Because they had guns and swords
3. Montezuma
4. Tenochtitlán
5. He thought Cortés would take it and leave.
6. The city was built on an island with temples, palaces, and towering pyramids.
7. Skilled warriors and talented builders
8. Cortés took over with more troops from Spain.

Unit 5 American Revolution
page 59

1. March 1765
2. A payment
3. Angry; Because they had no representation in the British government
4. They did not have a vote on taxes they had to pay.
5. They refused to buy British goods, burned stamps, didn't pay the tax, and destroyed buildings where the taxes were collected.
6. To end the rioting
7. So that colonists could not trade with other nations
8. Answers may vary. (Example: start of the American Revolution)

Unit 5 U.S. Constitution
page 63

1. A plan for a new government
2. Executive, legislative, judicial
3. Executive
4. They felt it was incomplete.
5. Anti-Federalists were against the Constitution and Federalists were for the Constitution.
6. They promised to put a list of rights in the Constitution.
7. Because the states ratified the Constitution
8. Changes that promise certain rights and freedoms.

Unit 5 Civil War
page 67

1. Slaves
2. To end
3. They could be attacked or arrested.
4. Runaway slaves
5. North to the free states and Canadian border
6. A conductor took slaves to the safe houses. The stationmasters owned the safe houses.
7. To help slaves escape quickly
8. Because the Fugitive Slave Law allowed slave catchers to take slaves back to the slave state they ran from

Answer Key

Unit 6 Life Science: Human Body
page 73

1. The spinal column
2. The cranium
3. Always wear a helmet.
4. The lower jaw
5. They stack on top of each other
6. Your back could not move.
7. Disks, ears, and nose
8. Protects the spinal cord

Unit 6 Physical Science: Chemistry
page 77

1. Matter is anything that has mass and takes up space. Examples may vary.
2. Physical changes
3. Molecules
4. They move faster.
5. Boiling water
6. Gas
7. The molecules move slower and slower.
8. More slowly

Unit 6 Earth Science: Water and Weather
page 81

1. The different effects of hurricanes
2. A hurricane is much more serious and larger than a thunderstorm.
3. June through November
4. Warm water and low air pressure
5. The atmosphere
6. The atmosphere pushes down with less force.
7. Destroyed homes, mudslides, or destroyed trees
8. It caused billions of dollars in damage and killed more than 1,000 people.

Unit 6 Earth Science: Rocks and Minerals
page 85

1. Answers may vary. (Examples: yellow, shiny, soft)
2. Answers may vary.
3. Because it can be hammered or pressed into different shapes
4. It doesn't easily combine with other elements.
5. Because gold does not dissolve or corrode
6. Earth's crust
7. Copper and silver
8. It can easily form into a wire.

Answer Key

Unit 7 Persuasive Letters I
page 93

1. Neither
2. Philadelphia
3. Believes war is evil
4. Fighting between people of the same country
5. Patriots want independence from England. Loyalists want to be a part of England.
6. Peaceful discussion
7. A person who believes there should be no government
8. To not take a side

Unit 7 Persuasive Letters II
page 97

1. Job
2. Students should be in school for more days of the year.
3. School children needed to work on their families' farms.
4. Child psychologists or doctors
5. One month of instruction lost
6. To strengthen his or her argument
7. Any two of the following: Computer, mathematical, technical, and health care fields
8. Japan

Unit 8 Book Review I
page 103

1. *Stuart Little*
2. E. B. White
3. Stuart Little
4. He can walk upright and talk.
5. He is very determined.
6. The plot has loose ends.
7. To give an opinion of *Stuart Little*
8. Answers may vary.

Unit 8 Film Review I
page 107

1. *Charlotte's Web* by E. B. White
2. A pig
3. Fern is more assertive in the movie.
4. Charlotte doesn't look real.
5. Because of the comic touches that have been added
6. Charlotte
7. Perfect
8. Answers may vary.

Answer Key

Unit 9 Advertisement I
page 113

1. Seven
2. You only have to brush your teeth once a week.
3. So that it stands out in the ad
4. To strip away
5. Mouth-friendly acids
6. To sell BLAST toothpaste
7. To help the reader relate to the ad
8. Answers may vary.

Unit 9 Advertisement II
page 117

1. A nondairy shake
2. Keep you healthy
3. It is nutritious.
4. Vitamins and minerals
5. Freezer
6. Improve your skin, hair, nails, and overall well-being
7. To relate to the reader
8. Answers may vary.

Unit 10 Speech I
page 123

1. The elected chair
2. Citizens of the town
3. Emergency health care in the town
4. The speaker's wife; she became ill suddenly
5. Heavy traffic
6. Because he wants the emergency clinic to be a part of it
7. With the mall
8. Answers may vary.

Unit 10 Speech II
page 127

1. Valley farmers
2. Farmer Laura for Farmer of the Year
3. To see her farming methods in action
4. The world would experience drought, terrible winds, rain, or flooding.
5. Farm equipment
6. People would starve.
7. Fossil fuel
8. Answers may vary.

Notes

Notes